How to Make Big Money in Small Apartments

How to Finally Earn the Money You Deserve in Real Estate Investing

By Lance A. Edwards

This publication is designed to provide accurate and authoritative information with regard to the subject matter covered. It is sold with the understanding that the publisher is not engaged in rendering legal, accounting, or other professional advice. If legal advice or other expert assistance is required, the services of a competent professional person should be sought.

The author, Lance Edwards, is available for a limited number of speaking engagements and consulting assignments. He also has a selection of training programs and mentoring programs. For information, contact Lance Edwards at 713-476-0102 or ClientCare@fcgllc.com.

Dedication

This book is first dedicated to the memory of my late wife, Eri Edwards. Eri supported me when I first made the decision to enter real estate part-time and then again when we together took the leap and I left the "security" of a 20 year job. Eri, you are missed every day.

Next, the book is dedicated to my daughter, Stephanie Edwards, without whom this book or the Case Studies described herein wouldn't exist. Stephanie is my original "Reason Why." She's why I got started in real estate and small apartments. From a deep desire to be able to fund the best education for Stephanie were the strategies and techniques contained in these pages developed.

Finally, I want to dedicate this book to the students, clients, partners and mentors who demonstrated to me over the past twelve years the power of the wealth creation methods revealed here.

Testimonials

Praise from the students you'll read about in this book, and others from the real estate industry:

"This book and the methods inside gives others the encouragement and necessary understandings to evolve their business and plan for retirement."

— Peter Arianas

"I've used the methods taught by the Lance Edwards team and now I have acquired multiple streams of income and my business has exploded."

— Delwin Marks

"Lance Edwards and his crew gave me the courage to always ask about deals and never pass on an opportunity."

— Scott Kodak

"Even the newest newbie can start today and make more money than they ever imagined within the first thirty days."

— Traci Williams

"Thanks to Lance Edwards, my business has completely shifted, and now I make three times the money for the same amount of work. The plan really works and I'm grateful to incorporate it into my business."

— Terri Attaway

"I've personally shared many of Lance's tips with my friends and colleagues and I'm thrilled to now be able to recommend a book that packs all of the tips into an individual source."

— Anil Sikri

Table of Contents

Summary of Case Studies

Chapter 5

Chapter 6

Chapter 7

Chapter 8

Chapter 9

Chapter 10

Foreword by Ron LeGrand

After hosting Lance Edwards' training webinars for years and having him as a client and friend, I was happy when I learned that he was coming out with his first book. And I was proud when he asked me to write this foreword.

Lance is the real deal and it's reflected in this book. In the pages you are about to read, Lance lays out the opportunities, strategies, myths, secrets and the internal obstacles for anyone interested in playing bigger in real estate thru multifamily.

I've always been impressed with comments from Lance's students that he gives away more information for FREE than others charge a deserved premium for. And true to form, he's held nothing back here.

The book covers everything from finding deals, funding deals and wholesaling apartments - while laying out all of the information in a logical and readily understandable format. I guess that's why he has a Case Study of how an 18 year old made $30,000 wholesaling a small apartment with his father in just 9 business days! If an 18 year old can do this following Lance's system, anyone can.

I've been doing and teaching real estate investing (or real estate *entrepreneurship* as Lance calls it) for more decades than I'd like to admit. I'm known as The Millionaire Maker and the one common thread that I've observed amongst the 5% that are massively successful in real estate is their ability to get past the internal head-talk, the junk we tell ourselves.

And so I was especially pleased that Lance devoted time to the head game or what he calls the mindset. It's critical for anyone getting started in real estate and certainly for anyone looking to play bigger in the world of apartments. The abundant Case Studies from his students and his own deals make the teachings real, understandable and entertaining while reconditioning your own mindset of what's possible for you.

For anyone just getting started in real estate, you can start in small apartments - just like Lance did - and all of the newbies cited in the Case Studies contained in these pages.

If you're currently doing houses, you need to consider adding small apartments to your profit stream. As Lance points out in the book, the same buyers who are buying your wholesale house deals will buy your small apartment deals. And the same private investors who are lending on houses will lend on small apartments. You'll just be making bigger money per transaction.

No matter your cash or credit situation, or your experience level, Lance demonstrates - and more importantly - gets you to understand and believe that you are qualified to play bigger and enter the world of small apartments today!

Finally, besides the criticality of mindset, Lance hits the nail on the head in pointing out that none of us are in the real estate business. We are all in the marketing business - just like any business. And we have an incredibly simple business model; we are always marketing for two things: deals and dollars.

This is a central and critical theme throughout the book because once you understand how to match-make other people's money with deals of any size, you break through the limiting beliefs that may be preventing you from playing bigger.

Lance further reinforces the point by showing precisely how to market for deals and dollars. The Case Study on the two unemployed partners who used the exact formula given in this book to raise $6 million to purchase four projects in 10 months is inspiring and educational.

Embrace Lance's teachings and wisdom here. And more importantly, act upon it.

Ron LeGrand

Chapter 1

Introduction / What's in it For You?

I would like to first thank you for taking the time to read this book. Because you are committing your time and your trust in me to "deliver the goods," I have committed that this book deliver to you, the reader, meaningful content. In it, I reveal the street-wise strategies to growing your wealth and cash flow through your very own apartment business.

This collaboration will teach you the proper steps and hopefully answer all of your questions. With that in mind, let the training begin.

What's In It for You?

By reading this book, you will learn what took me several years in the time it takes you to read a couple hundred pages. Here's just a sampling of what you'll learn:

- How to pay your rent or mortgage for one year by wholesaling one small apartment contract per year
- How to create financial freedom in five years or less using none of your own cash or credit

- How to find the real deals
- How to raise all of the private money you want for real estate using none of your own cash or credit
- Five ways to get started in apartments of any size (and 16 strategies unique to small apartments)
- How to condition your mindset for Playing Bigger

So who is Lance Edwards?

My Story

It's absolutely vital that I share my background with you so you can understand the process and know my journey through real estate investing over the past 10+ years. You see, I eat my own cookin'.

In 2001, I had a young family with a wife and daughter. I worked for a publicly-traded software company which means that you live and die by the stock price and the company's quarterly performance. You are only as good as your current quarter.

The company had enjoyed a high rise but the over-exuberance was starting to have its effect - like a hangover following a big party. The company was conducting what they then called "RIF's" or "Reductions-in-Force." I worked 60 hours per week in a position where if I missed my quarterly numbers, I was summarily fired.

It was a little bit of a pressure cooker and that, combined with seeing my friends "RIF'ed," led me to searching for a "Plan B" or an additional income stream as financial security for my young family. That's how I discovered real estate.

In 2002, I took on my very first real estate training, which was a teleseminar on how to buy houses with no money down. Taught by a well-known national instructor, the program delivered world-class training in the form of priceless wisdom, which I am now privileged to share with you today but applied to apartments.

My trainer shared a special bit of knowledge with me that changed the trajectory of my life. To begin, he said, "You know, I made a lot of money doing houses. But I came to realize that to meet my financial goals, I needed to shift to multifamily."

I repeat: "Multifamily."

He concluded, "Multifamily provides bigger numbers in a shorter time period." That statement just made all the sense in the world to me, and that idea quickly transitioned my thought process on the real estate business as a whole.

After that training session, I came out with a hunger to find small apartments of my own in order to make the most money in the shortest amount of time. In fact, my first deal was a small apartment - known as a four-plex - which I was able to purchase with no money down, just like I learned in the training.

Let me tell you, there is nothing like your first deal. It is without a shadow of a doubt, the most critical deal in your real estate career. Above all else, your first deal is critical because it not only proves that the system works, but more importantly, it proves that the system works for you.

The nanosecond after you walk out from closing your first deal, your brain automatically jumps to ask yourself: "How can I do more of these?" And that first deal was the launching pad to my real estate business. After closing my first deal, I not only had a sense of satisfaction, but I also had the additional confidence needed to make additional deals. At the time, I was only working real estate on a part-time basis, and every second was vital for success.

With a very demanding full-time corporate job, I was still able to close 50 nothing-down deals over two and a half years working part-time, closing on both multi-family and single family deals. Overall, I bought another four-plex, then a 10-unit property, 50-unit property, 56-unit property, and an 85-unit project - always, always, always using other people's money (OPM), because that is the method that I was taught.

Working small apartments part-time for 3 years allowed me to walk into my boss' office on a Friday morning and hand him a slip of paper that essentially said, "I'm done. I don't need this anymore."

There are few feelings as powerful as those that come from being able to tell your boss that you are done with your job and that you no longer require a nine-to-five to pay your bills. No more alarm clocks. No more working to build someone else's dream instead of my own.

At this point, I had been working within the corporate realm for 20 years with the same company. After such a long commitment, my boss could not help but ask, "Lance, can you tell me how you are able to leave?" The answer to that question lies within the text of this book.

For those of you hoping to leave your j-o-b, I'm here to show you how. An important aside, however: never leave your job until you have a side business up and running that can replace the lost income. Throughout these pages, you are invited to learn how to earn supplemental or replacement income from your current job.

I left my job in 2005 and never looked back. Using other people's money, I was out doing deals: buying and holding, or just plain flipping apartments and apartment contracts. After a few years, some curious folks from my real estate club approached me and asked me to teach them the secrets of my success.

In July of 2007, I began to show others how to make deals without using their own hard earned cash. I held my first training seminar and launched the teaching side of my business, which is how many people know me today.

In the process, I've discovered that I have two passions: deal-making and teaching. And there's no greater satisfaction for me than helping a student get their first apartment deal done – which I do as my daily vocation, with students across the country. The largest deal I've done to date with a student is an $11 million 294 unit apartment deal.

Perhaps we will do an apartment deal together.

My Mantra

So let me go ahead and tell you my mantra which is emphasized throughout the book, *"You do not have to graduate from single family to multifamily. You can start with multifamily."* This book is that proof and recipe.

My Assumptions

If you are reading this book, I know that we are kindred spirits. Perhaps you are like I was in 2002: just starting out as a newbie. Or maybe you are experienced in real estate but aching to play bigger. Regardless, I know some of the following are true of you:

- You want to play bigger
- You want immediate cash, or passive income, or both
- You are an employee and you want to leave your job
- You own a small business and you are looking for a retirement plan
- You have an existing real estate business and you want to scale-up
- You are worried about funding your kids' college education
- You have skepticism (and probably fear) about getting started in apartments
- You are concerned that you are not qualified due to financial constraints, credit constraints or lack of experience
- You believe there is a better way.

If you fit at least one of these criteria (and I know you do), you are in the right place. The above parameters describe me when I started and those who I work with every day.

Case Study – His Retirement Plan Was to "Drop Dead"

Dan Badinghaus is a small business owner with a construction company. He's also one of my Circle of Champions members (people who've closed their first apartment deal). Dan flipped his first small apartment deal with his 18 year old son, Dylan, and made $30,000 in 9 business days (the record so far amongst my students).

When I interviewed him about the deal, Dan said something that really struck me at my core. He said, "Prior to getting involved with you and apartments, I thought my retirement plan was me dropping dead on the job site."

Wow. That speaks to the power of what you are learning here and a reason why I teach. In the pages to follow, there will be more on how Dan and Dylan made $30,000 on their first small apartment deal – and others just like them.

Bonus Resource
Interview: *Circle of Champions Roundtable Interview*
www.BMSABook.com/roundtable

Four Components of Success in Real Estate

I want to begin by revealing something that you've probably not been told about real estate - the *Real Estate Success Model,* depicted here in the triangle. I am introducing it here and will explain it in detail in Chapter 9.

4 Components of
Real Estate Success™

There are four components of success in real estate, which will be reemphasized throughout the book:

- **Component #1**: Specialized Knowledge
- **Component #2**: Marketing
- **Component #3**: Systems
- **Component #4**: Mindset

Component #1: Specialized Knowledge

This is the "how to" of the apartment business: how to find deals, analyze them, negotiate them, flip them, buy them, fund them, improve them, sell them, etc. It is essential to success but NOT sufficient for success. You need more than knowledge. If knowledge were enough, librarians would be billionaires.

Component #2: Marketing

Peter Drucker, the esteemed master on entrepreneurship summarized it best. Business is nothing but marketing and innovation. Everything else is just a cost center. If your phone is not ringing, you don't have a business; you have a hobby.

Therefore, you are NOT in the real estate business. You are in the marketing business. Marketing is everything. In fact, two-thirds of your time needs to be devoted to marketing.

You see, our business model is incredibly simple. We constantly market for two things: deals and dollars.

What do I mean by deals? Deals are properties which I can get control of under preferred terms: discounted price, flexible financing terms, or both.

The other side of the marketing equation is the dollars. And by dollars, I mean finding buyers or investors. If I'm wholesaling a property, I need to find a buyer. If I'm looking to buy and hold on a property for passive income and appreciation, I seek out private investors for cash and/or credit.

On one hand, I find the deals. On the other hand I find the dollars. And I match-make the two. We are simply matchmakers.

Now, before I leave the second success component of marketing, I need to point out that there's a third thing we market for when we buy and hold apartments: residents (tenants). They provide us passive income and net worth.

I don't like the term "tenant" because it tends to carry a derogatory connotation. Residents are those enlightened souls who live in our buildings and go to work each day so that they can give us 40% of their income as rent. Those who don't pay are "tenants."

Component #3: Systems

Let me tell you right now that I don't want you to take this information and go create another job for yourself where you wake up one morning and realize you work for a lunatic boss – yourself. You know, that boss who is constantly on your back and never satisfied.

You avoid this trap by building a business with automated systems that replicate your personal efforts in a predictable way. Systems have three parts: 1) Processes, 2) People and 3) Technology.

Now I realize that you may be starting out as I did – as a solopreneur. You're the proverbial chief bottle washer and CEO.

That's perfectly fine. BUT I do want you to have the vision to establish those systems one-by-one as they will be explained here.

Which systems do you begin with? Well, since two-thirds of your activities should be devoted to marketing, your initial concentration should be on creating your marketing systems.

Component #4: Mindset

This final component is the most important. In fact, I believe it's 70% of your success in real estate. You see, the chief obstacle between each of us and our grandest ambition is FEAR. No one wants to talk about it but I make it a center stone to my training approach.

By mindset, I mean the ability to take action despite fear; the ability to take action when we don't feel like it. Mindset also means having the ability to confidently play BIGGER. It does NOT mean that the fear goes away. It'll always be there in some form. But successful entrepreneurs learn how to act through it.

The good news is that mindset is a learnable skill. And in Chapter 10, I'll show you how to develop the mindset of playing bigger – skills that I learned and teach daily.

Bonus Resource
Webinar: *The Whole Truth about Real Estate Investing*
www.BMSABook.com/truth

Small vs. Mid-size vs. Large Apartments

This book is titled, How to Make Big Money in Small Apartments. And while I will reveal 16 strategies that are unique to small apartments, everything else is directly portable and scalable to mid-size and large apartments. Everything.

So why do I emphasize small apartments? Because of mindset. You see, if I were to title this book, "How to Make Big Money in Apartments," your subconscious would probably jump to an image of a 200 unit apartment building that maybe you once lived in. And your little voice would say, "I can't do that."

Yet, when I add the word "small" to apartments, it all of a sudden becomes plausible. Your little voice says, "I could do small apartments." And that is just one reason why I encourage you to begin with small apartments (more reasons in the next chapter).

Get that critical first small apartment deal done and then the larger deals miraculously appear possible.

What You Can Expect

I've organized this book in a number of ways to facilitate your predominant learning style. We all learn in different modes so I've included not only the written text but visual and audio teaching methodologies.

Chapters - This book is split into chapters according to skills and techniques. There are several methods necessary to study in order to succeed in real estate, and each chapter will let you know exactly what to do.

Chapter Summary - For those who like to peruse, a Chapter Summary is found at the end of each chapter, along with an explanation of what's coming next. The book is intended to be read from beginning to end but you can certainly pull nuggets from each chapter to put to use.

Case Studies - Additionally, since we learn through stories, there are over 40 case studies that illustrate how normal people with no prior real estate experience were able to utilize the methods I teach and earn enormous amounts of money that they initially thought improbable. These Case Studies are drawn from my Circle of Champions members, who have closed at least one apartment deal, or from my very own personal experiences.

Frequently Asked Questions – The entire book is dedicated to teaching and answering your questions. In the last chapter, I summarize the most frequently asked questions - with a reference to the chapter where the topic is discussed.

Glossary - Like all industries, the real estate industry utilizes its own jargon and acronyms so I've included a Glossary at the end of the book as a handy reference as you learn these strategies. It's comprehensive. Use it.

Bonus Resources - Finally, throughout the book, you'll find additional learning resources in the *multimedia* format of tools, reports, and webinars; where you can drill down into additional detail on a topic of interest. There are also interviews between the successful students you'll meet in the book and me. The webinars are conducted by me and my hand-selected experts where you learn and have your questions answered. At the back of the book, you'll find a summary of the Bonus Resources.

Bonus Resource
Webinar: *How to Make Big Money in Small Apartments*
www.BMSABook.com/bmsa

The first portion of the book is devoted to the theme of *"Why You Should Be in Small Apartments."* The balance of the book explains, *"How to Get Started in Small Apartments."*

You Need a Mentor

I'm going to tell you right now that if you are serious about this business and playing BIG, you need a mentor. Every success has had mentors.

I'm offering to mentor you – whether thru the form of this book and me sharing over a decade of lessons learned, or more formally in working with you weekly. Either way, if you truly want the fast track in playing BIG, find a mentor.

Bonus Resource
Complimentary Planning Session
www.BMSABook.com/plan

You have the ability to create a life for yourself that will let you retire years, if not decades, sooner than you'd thought possible. If you use the knowledge provided in this book, I can help you make that happen.

Coming Up

In the next chapter, you are going to discover the *7 Keys to Building a Real Estate Empire* and how small apartments are the IDEAL vehicle for getting you started.

Chapter Summary

- Your first apartment deal is your most critical deal – for confidence. That's why I recommend small apartments to start.
- You don't need to graduate from single family to multifamily. You can start with multifamily – just like I did and my students do.
- What is true for small apartments applies to mid-size and large apartments.
- There are four components to success in real estate which are all covered throughout the book:
  1. Specialized Knowledge
  2. Marketing
  3. Systems
  4. Mindset
- You are not in the real estate business. You are in the marketing business.
- You always market for two things: deals and dollars. When you own property, you also market for residents.
- You need a mentor and I'm offering to be it.

Bonus Resources Summary

Interview: *Circle of Champions Roundtable Interview*
www.BMSABook.com/roundtable

Webinar: *How to Make Big Money in Small Apartments*
www.BMSABook.com/bmsa

Complimentary Planning Session
www.BMSABook.com/plan

Chapter 2

Why Small Apartments?

I n this chapter, I want to pay forward what my first real estate mentor did for me when he told me to get started with apartments. I'm going to explain all of the advantages to you in getting started with small apartments while teaching you the *7 Keys to Building a Real Estate Empire*.

I learned the *7 Keys to Building a Real Estate Empire* very early in my career, and I'm fortunate to share these keys and pay it forward. Doing deals has its own level of excitement, but helping others close their first deal is a whole new level of delight.

In order to begin on the subject of small apartments, I think it's enlightening to first contrast small apartments as a wealth creation vehicle versus houses.

State of House Investing Today

Many people begin in real estate by purchasing or flipping single-family houses. That's fine, but once you are exposed to my *7 Keys to Building a Real Estate Empire*, you are going to see that multifamily is the way to go.

And if you are active in house investing today, you've probably experienced the challenges I hear when I speak across the country to real estate entrepreneurs who come to me looking for a better way to go in real estate.

For example, today, hedge funds are buying up houses in bulk. These hedge funds are gobbling up the big portfolios from the banks, which decreases the amount of deals available to individual buyers while simultaneously decreasing profit margins. It is not uncommon to have multiple bidders on a single house with prices that are basically outside of the profitable zone.

In addition, the Dodd-Frank Law (which went into effect in 2014) and placed restrictions on seller financing for _owner-occupied_ properties has made it increasingly challenging for real estate investors to sell houses with owner-financing – one of the tried and true strategies for passive income.

In summary, single family deal flow has tightened; competition has increased with multiple bidders per house, and profits have shrunk. That, combined with the new Dodd-Frank hurdles, has a lot of house entrepreneurs wondering what to do. Let's contrast that with the world of apartments – where I work.

State of Apartment Investing Today

First of all, small and mid-sized apartments are gold mines that are untouched by hedge funds.

Hedge funds traditionally buy large, apartment complexes because they must move huge chunks of money—anywhere from $3 million to hundreds of millions per transaction. That's why they are now buying houses in bulk, because they can move large sums of money with the purchase of a single portfolio of houses.

In between those multi-million dollar house portfolio deals and large apartment complexes, there is a revolving door of small and mid-size apartments left for us entrepreneurs to work with. You see, the hedge funds see this marketplace of small and mid-size apartments as inefficient because they can't buy up six-plexes or ten-plexes in bulk like they can with houses. The realm of small to mid-size apartments is the realm of the individual entrepreneur.

But even given the state of house investing, there is still very little competition in small or mid-size apartments because most people focus on houses and carry the notion that they must graduate into apartments, or that they need big cash and credit, or that they'll have to deal with tenants and toilets. All of these are false notions (as I'll explain in the next chapter).

Apartments are the IDEAL Investment

One of the early things my first mentor taught me before he taught me real estate is how to evaluate different investment vehicles by the IDEAL formula, which is an acronym for the perfect investment. The perfect investment has five attributes:

- Income
- Depreciation
- Equity
- Appreciation
- Leverage

Income – The IDEAL investment generates passive income; with the key word being passive, meaning that it generates "mailbox money" without your active involvement.

Depreciation - The IDEAL investment enjoys the IRS tax benefits of depreciation. Depreciation is a "paper loss" that the IRS allows to be deducted from your active income which you pay tax on. It is possible to completely (and legally) offset your income tax liability from active income by owning a sufficient amount of income-producing real estate. There are multiple strategies just on this one attribute.

Bonus Resource
Webinar: *Real Estate Tax Strategies Your CPA Doesn't Know*
www.BMSABook.com/taxes

Equity – The IDEAL investment has growing equity over time. Equity is the difference between the value of the property and any underlying mortgages. Increased equity comes from your residents paying down your mortgage balance thru their rent payments.

That increased equity is captured as cash when you either: 1) sell the property or 2) refinance the property with a new loan and convert the increased equity to cash (tax free) – perhaps to buy more income producing real estate.

Appreciation – The IDEAL investment increases in value over time – thru 1) market appreciation or 2) forced appreciation or 3) both. And that also translates into increased equity - which can be harvested as cash. Forced appreciation is explained in Chapter 5.

Leverage – The final attribute of the IDEAL investment is that you can amplify its yield thru leverage, i.e. use other people's money (OPM) to purchase it.

Let's examine this IDEAL formula across 4 different investment vehicles to discover that a commercial income-producing property – like an apartment building – is the only vehicle that possesses all five attributes.

Comparison of Investment Vehicles				
	Apts	**Business**	**Stocks**	**Bonds**
Income	✓	✓	Some	✓
Depreciation	✓			
Equity	✓	✓	✓	✓
Appreciation	✓	✓	✓	Some
Leverage	✓	✓	✓	

Vehicle 1: Apartments - Let's start with the vehicle of apartments. Do they have passive income? Yes, from rents and the use of management companies. Do they offer the tax benefits of depreciation? Yes, lots. Do they contain equity? Absolutely. And it grows even if there is no appreciation, thanks to monthly

mortgage balance pay-down. That equity is in the form of land and the improved value of the buildings.

Is appreciation present in apartments? Yes, thru market appreciation, forced appreciation or both. Can we purchase them thru leverage? Of course. In fact, that's a key wealth creating attribute of real estate.

Vehicle 2: Business - What about owning a business? Does a business have passive income? Yes, if it is run by managers and not by you. Does a business offer depreciation? No, not really other than the small value of depreciation on the office equipment (there is depreciation if it is a heavy industry and there's lots of physical equipment).

Does the business offer equity? Yes, if it is managed by others; it can be sold or refinanced. Does a business have appreciation? Yes, if the net profits are growing and, again, it's managed by others. Can we use leverage to buy a business? Yes, again if it has true passive income. If it's really just another form of a job by the owner, none of these latter attributes apply.

Vehicle 3: Stocks – Do stocks pay income? Yes, if the company pays a dividend. No, if not. Does a stock provide you the tax benefit of depreciation? No, that's applied to the company which sold you the shares.

Is there equity in stock? Yes, you can borrow against the value of your stock. Does a stock offer appreciation? Yes, at least you hope so. Can you leverage a stock portfolio? Yes, your brokerage company will loan you money against the value of your stock (called margin loans and generally limited to 50% of the value) to pull out cash or buy other stock.

Vehicle 4: Bonds – Finally, is there income from owning bonds? Yes, absolutely. That is the primary reason for their existence. Do bonds offer you depreciation tax benefits? No. Is their equity in your bonds? Yes, but it's generally fixed to your original investment amount.

Do bonds offer appreciation? Yes, they can if interest rates drop but appreciation is generally not a primary reason the routine investor buys bonds. Can you leverage your bond portfolio and pull cash-out? No, not normally.

So, when you line them up, you see that apartments are the IDEAL investment vehicle with five ways of improving your financial position. In just a few moments, I'll also outline a sixth way of utilizing apartments: wholesaling.

Start with Small Apartments

Based on the above IDEAL formula, I selected apartments at the outset as my primary investment vehicle to financial independence for my family. But before you start thinking, *"Wow, I'll go do one large apartment deal and be financially free,"* let me inject some experience from mentoring hundreds.

The most important thing is for you to get that critical first apartment deal done. It's all a matter of mindset, which I explained in Chapter 1 and will further discuss in Chapter 10. With that first deal comes confidence. And let me tell you, small apartments close faster, typically 30 days. When we closed our $11 million deal, it closed in 5 months and 28 days – and it was ahead of schedule! That's too long a time for your mindset and little voice to conjure up all the reasons your first deal won't close.

Also, with small apartments, there's smaller dollar amounts involved. There's less money to raise. A single private investor can fund your purchase. And when it comes to wholesaling, there's lots of readily identified buyers of small apartments (think of all the burned-out single family landlords - more on this later).

For these reasons, I recommend *beginning* with small apartments. Then you can scale up to mid-size and large apartments as your confidence is cemented with that critical first deal. Or you can do lots of small apartment deals.

So how do I define small apartments? There's no official definition but here's how I define it: <u>a small apartment is a building with 2 to 30 units</u>. However, I need to make a clarification. Any multifamily dwelling smaller than a five-unit building is *residential* and 5+ units is *commercial*. So 2-4 unit properties (duplexes, triplexes and four-plexes) are defined as small apartments but are considered residential.

The reason for this distinction is because residential properties are valued based on *"comparable prices,"* while commercial property valuations are purely based on the property's *"financials,"* it's net operating income (NOI). I will explain this in detail in Chapter 5.

One more point. Maybe, you are asking, "But what about the Dodd-Frank Law with apartments?" Good question. The Dodd-Frank Law is not applicable to duplexes and higher as long as they are not "owner occupied," which is the case for most duplexes, triplexes, four-plexes, and 5+ unit apartment buildings. The keyword is "owner-occupied."

You see, the Dodd-Frank Law was written as a Consumer Protection Act to protect home owners from the lending abuses that led to the 2008 credit meltdown. If your buyer does not intend to occupy the building, there are no restrictions to owner financing a small apartment building (which is great news for buying, selling and flipping apartments).

How Most People Start in Real Estate – Wholesaling

The Glossary provides a definition of wholesaling but since this is a great strategy for so many doing their first deal in real estate, it's important that I explain it here to ensure we are on the same page.

DEFINITION: *Wholesaling is the process of placing an apartment under contract to purchase and then selling your contract at a higher price to another End-Buyer who closes on the property and pays you a handsome "assignment fee" – which is the difference between your contract price and the price they are willing to pay. No real estate license is required.*

You simply assign your position as the buyer on the contract to another buyer in exchange for dollars (typically 5 figures on small apartment deals). The key is to place a purchase contract on the apartment at a discounted price, or with flexible financing terms, or both. Many of my students start out this way. It generates chunks of cash.

As a wholesaler, you never take title to the property. You don't use any of your own money; your End-Buyer does that. They provide the down payment and loan approval. You get a check at closing. It's also known as "flipping the contract."

While some use the term "flipping" to mean buying a property, rehabbing it and then selling it at a higher price to a buyer, I use the term "flipping" interchangeably with "wholesaling." Throughout the book, wholesaling means flipping the contract and applies to small, mid-size and large apartments.

Many people who are familiar with wholesaling houses don't even realize you can wholesale apartments. Of course you can. You can wholesale anything.

Case Study - $24,000 from Her First Small Apartment Flip

Terri Attaway is a realtor of 30 years. She's done countless single family deals BUT for other people, as an agent, where she was getting paid a modest commission by the seller. She decided it was time to do some deals for herself and make much more money.

Terri found two triplexes that were totally vacant and needed rehab. The owner didn't have the money to do the rehab. Terri placed the properties under contract to purchase, with herself as the buyer. She then found a rehabber who was looking to "move up" to small apartments and assigned her two contracts to him. Her End-Buyer put up the funding for purchase and closed on the deal. Terri received a check for $24,000 at closing! It was her largest check received for any deal she'd ever done. Now she is shifting her business from houses to small apartments.

Bonus Resource
Interview: *$24,000 from Her First Small Apartment Flip*
www.BMSABook.com/triplexes

There's A Better Way than Starting from Scratch Each Day

When starting in real estate, most people start with wholesaling houses. They find a house, then a buyer, and then they repeat the process. Generally the assignment fee for a house is somewhere between $2,000 and $5,000, which - in my opinion - seems like too much work for a small profit.

While many people can start from scratch in the manner listed above, it's as if you never move past starting from scratch.

You see, after flipping a house, these sellers are then forced to start completely over. Despite having more knowledge on the subject, these flippers quickly get burned out and drop out of the business after a few deals, feeling as if their time was wasted in many of the scenarios.

It's possible to make some quick cash starting from scratch over and over but that is no way to build an empire. That is just a way to grind until you give up. Instead, let's focus on making more money with the same effort and how working with apartments can set you apart from the pack.

With that in mind, let's move on to the *7 Keys to Building a Real Estate Empire*.

7 Keys to Building a Real Estate Empire

There are 7 keys to building your real estate empire. I will explain them here and revisit and reinforce them throughout the rest of the book – all in the context of why small apartments are the perfect place for you to start:

- **Key #1:** Marketing, Marketing, Marketing
- **Key #2:** Close Your First Deal

- **Key #3:** Pick a Niche That is in Demand
- **Key #4:** Leverage Your Activity
- **Key #5:** Do Larger and Larger Deals
- **Key #6:** Use Passive Income and Appreciation to Buy More Assets
- **Key #7:** Use Other People's Money

Bonus Resource
Webinar: *7 Keys to Building a Real Estate Empire*
www.BMSABook.com/7keys

Let's examine each of the 7 keys.

Key #1: Marketing, Marketing, Marketing

As I pointed out in Chapter 1, we are not in the real estate business; we are in the *marketing* business. Real estate just happens to be the product. While marketing is listed as the first component, it really ties into each of these 7 keys. If your phone isn't ringing, you don't have a business, you have a hobby.

Our business model in real estate is incredibly simple because we focus on marketing for three things:

1. Deals
2. Dollars
3. Residents

That is our business - whether wholesaling or buying to hold. On one hand, you are marketing to find *deals*, and on the other hand, you are marketing to find *dollars*. This is the standard whether you are doing small single-family deals or 300-unit buildings. It's all about *deals and dollars*.

You create deal flow by constantly searching for motivated sellers or distressed situations in real estate.

When wholesaling a real estate deal, finding the dollars simply means that you find a *buyer*. When you hang on to a deal, finding the dollars means finding a private investor who will invest in your project; your role will be that of an overseer, an asset manager, where you receive passive income and/or appreciation.

Finally, on your buy and hold properties, you are marketing to find *residents*. The ability to keep an apartment full with paying residents is how you create ongoing cash flow and increased equity - due to forced appreciation (explained in Chapter 5).

Remember, cash and cash flow comes from marketing for **deals**, **dollars**, and **residents**. What is the second key?

Key #2: Close Your First Deal

There is no more critical deal than your first apartment deal. This was true for me as it will be true for you. It provides you the confidence and mindset that not only does this business work, it works for you.

Olive Jar Model

I had another mentor, a large apartment developer, who revealed to me what I call the Olive Jar Model. He explained that closing your first deal is like getting the first olive out of the jar — getting the first one out is difficult, but once you get the first one out, the rest just seem to fall out. It'll be the same with your apartment business.

And that is one of the reasons why I encourage people to start by *wholesaling*. Let's examine some other reasons why I recommend wholesaling small apartments as a start:

- There are lots of small apartments to prospect from
- There are lots of buyers of small apartments
- Small apartments close fast, generally 30 days
- Owner financing is common with small apartments

What do I mean by owner financing? I mean transactions where the owner agrees to receive some or all of their purchase in monthly installment payments. They act as the bank; there is no conventional lender involved.

Even if the owner has an existing bank loan in place, they can still sell their property thru owner financing. The slowest step in any real estate purchase is the bank financing. Remove that impediment and you close more deals faster. Just think... how many more buyers could you sell to if there was no bank qualifying required? Lots. Wholesaling combined with owner financing is the fastest path to a big payday for your first deal (and subsequent deals).

I say there are lots of small apartment buyers. Who are they?

Who are the Small Apartment Buyers?

First, **burned-out <u>single-family landlords</u>** are one of the biggest buying groups of small apartments. They are looking for passive income, and they have gotten tired of managing houses. They have come to realize the amount of work involved in managing scattered houses, and they "upgrade" into small apartments so they can hire management companies and exit the property management business.

Think about it. Would you rather oversee 10 houses or one 10-unit apartment building? In the next chapter, I'll explain how and why you should never self-manage your properties and show how small apartments afford you that capability, unlike houses.

If you are currently wholesaling houses to wanna-be landlords or house rehabbers who fix up and resell, you should definitely add small apartments to your wholesaling business. You can flip small apartments to the same investors who are buying your house deals, with bigger pay days. It'll add a new profit center, while leveraging your existing buyer relationships.

In addition, another large buying group of small apartments is **small business owners,** who are looking to exit the rat race. Most small business owners come to realize that they do not own a business—they own a full-time job. Their business does not exist without them and they see passive income from apartments as their escape vehicle.

These two groups (single family landlords and small business owners) are easily accessible. Therefore, it's simply the matter of finding the deals, finding the dollars, and bringing everything together so everyone wins.

Case Study – 10-Unit Building Sells in 22 Days

I once sold a 10-unit, owner-financed apartment that closed in 22 days without a bank. The buyer was a single family landlord who owned three rental houses and wanted to "move up" to small apartments. He was also an in-state truck driver and his plan was to live in one of the apartments. His wife would oversee the property while he was on the road. He also intended to use some of the adjoining land to park his truck and avoid the parking fees he paid someone else, while also leasing parking space to his other truck driver friends. He would have multiple income streams.

I sold it with owner-financing using what's called a *"wrap-around mortgage."* I received $27,000 cash at closing and $2,400 per month. I was the bank. More on how this works in Chapter 3.

Let's shift to Key #3 and see why apartments are hot.

Key #3: Pick a Niche in Demand

Just as with restaurants, the secret to success in business is to choose a niche that feeds the starving crowd. Go where the demand is.

The Rental Market Has Absolutely Exploded

The unfortunate truth is that in the aftermath of the housing collapse, many people are still in dire straits. Many can't qualify for a home loan. Others lost their homes to foreclosure. Many more lost so much money that they can't put enough down to buy a home. Consequently, homeownership fell off a cliff and there are a TON of renters right now. The demand for rental properties is sky high.

Combine that demand with lower rates of new apartment construction over the past several years of the Great Recession and we get a staggering imbalance between the number of people wanting to rent, and the places available for rent. Tenancy rates are off the charts and rents are at all-time highs.

For anyone in the apartment business – like you and me – this is a tremendously lucrative scenario, whether you intend to wholesale, buy and hold or rehab and resell.

For buy and hold players, the *passive income streams from owning apartments are much more secure and much larger than they have ever been.* Rents and occupancy are high and interest rates are at lifetime lows which mean that the cash flow per door is at levels unseen for decades.

For wholesalers, you have the opportunity to place yourself in the toll gate position of finding the deals and matching them to the high demand from the dollars, i.e. the buyers, for larger wholesaling fees. Choose the hot areas and you enjoy markets where apartment buyers are paying premium prices for even the so-so properties.

For rehabbers, you can find the distressed apartment properties; inject some rehab and improved management to raise the occupancy and/or rents and you'll reap the rewards of forced appreciation by selling at premium prices or refinancing at higher appraised values to pull cash out. Or just hang on to the properties for great cash flow and equity creation.

It's time for you to play bigger and take advantage of this enhanced demand created by the Great Recession. Apartments are the hot niche and *small apartments* are the place to start.

Key #4: Leverage Every Activity

Real estate creates more millionaires than any other pursuit because of the leverage involved. There's leverage of financial capital and leverage of human capital. In Key #7, I'll explain leverage of financial capital. In this Key #4, I'll point out how to leverage your human capital: your know-how and your time.

Above, I pointed out that most newbies approach real estate by wholesaling houses, which is fine. But, sadly, they start from scratch every single day. You have to be more strategic. I hear many people complain they don't have the time to do this. They do have the time - they're just not strategic in how they use it.

Recall from my story in Chapter 1 that when I started, I worked 60 hours per week in a job where I was summarily fired if I missed my quarterly numbers. No one has less time than I had when I started. And I chose apartments because when I looked at how I spent my time, I saw that apartments offer strategic time leverage.

And it has to do with how apartments are evaluated, in comparison to houses.

Apartments Are Based on the Numbers

You see, the value of a house is based on comparable prices, which is *subjective*. You have to examine the property as it would appear to a homeowner and *compare* pricing with other houses that are selling in the neighborhood. It generally requires a physical examination of the property prior to making an offer.

In contrast, apartments are based on the numbers, the financials. Give me an apartment Profit and Loss statement and a Rent Roll, and I can evaluate any apartment, sight unseen. I can evaluate deals at night. I can make an offer from my kitchen table, or anywhere I have fax or computer access, without seeing the property.

Evaluating apartments is the same as evaluating a business. In fact, apartments are businesses that just happen to be secured by physical real estate. It's all based on something called the net operating income (NOI), which I explain in detail in Chapter 5. But simply, the higher the NOI, the more the property is worth.

If you were looking to buy a business and someone called to tell you they had a business for sale, would you immediately jump in your car to go look at the office? No, the first thing you'd do is ask to look at the financials. You'd make an offer to purchase based on the profit and loss. It's the same with apartments.

This income-based evaluation approach also means that, with apartments, you can choose any market anywhere in the country. You just need to see the financials. You don't need to examine a property until it's under contract and you're in the phase called the due diligence period. And during that period, if you find anything you don't like, you can exit the deal with no penalty. Repeat... NO penalty.

It's the same if you are doing deals with 5 units or 300 units. It's all the same process. Remember, I encourage you to start small though.

This is how you can be strategic with your time. You evaluate financials on your time and you make offers from anywhere to anywhere. You can start with small apartments and then scale up to *lots* of small apartments, or to mid-size and larger apartments. You make more money per deal. That's the strategic time leverage afforded you through apartments.

Case Study – House Flipper Doubles Profits with Four-Plex

Delwin Marks wholesaled houses for 10 years before he decided to leverage his activities by getting started with apartments. He typically made $2,000 to $5,000 per house deal amidst heavy competition, with his largest profit of $7,000 on a single transaction. He found a four-plex for sale which he placed under contract. And when I interviewed Delwin about this Success Story, he explained that this property was located in the "hood."

Now, most people wouldn't consider doing a deal in the hood and I don't necessarily recommend it but nevertheless this property was in a rough area. And Delwin needed to find a buyer for this flip. So where do you find a buyer of a four-plex in the hood? Simple.

Delwin followed my teaching that the largest buying group of small apartments is single family landlords. So he put together a small direct mail campaign targeted to single family landlords who owned houses in the immediate vicinity of the four-plex. He explained that he had a four-plex for sale near their house and invited interested parties to call.

Think about it, owners of rental houses in the hood already know the area and are presumably comfortable with it. They could be interested in owning larger properties in the same neighborhood. Sure enough, Delwin got a call from a rental house owner near his four-plex who wanted to "move up" to apartments. Delwin flipped his contract and made $11,000 on a property in the hood – double the profit of his typical house deal.

Bonus Resource
Interview: *House Flipper Doubles Profits with Four-Plex*
www.BMSABook.com/double

This leads to Key #5: larger deals.

Key #5: Do Larger and Larger Deals

When I first started examining different types of businesses, I realized that there are just two business models:

1. High volume business
2. High ticket business

A high volume business is one where you have a high volume of transactions, with small to modest profit per transaction. There's also a high volume of activity. McDonald's operates this way. They've sold a jillion hamburgers based on high volume and very detailed systems. It's all based on volume.

A high ticket business is one where you deal in high-priced items. You make a high profit per transaction but there are fewer transactions per year. And there's a lower volume of activity.

These two business models are for any type of business. Then I learned about real estate wholesaling, the method of finding a property, placing it under contract and selling my contract to an End-Buyer. And I liked that model as a way to start. So I decided to make a business plan for it.

That plan aimed to make $100,000 in the first year. In the real estate trainings, they taught me to expect $3,000 to $5,000 per house flip. So, assuming I made $5,000 per house, I did the math and that meant 20 house deals a year, translating to about two deals per month. I'd have to find more than two deals per month, find two buyers per month and close two deals per month. Starting on a part-time basis with a full-time job, I knew I didn't have that kind of time.

Instead I asked, *"What if I made $50,000 per deal?"* I would only need two deals a year to hit my goal of $100,000. And that's another reason I decided to start with apartments. The higher-ticket price on these commercial properties meant greater leverage of my time. Bigger numbers would move me faster toward my financial goals.

Now let me ask you... Where do you think there is less competition? A high volume business or a high ticket business? If you said high ticket, you are correct. Let's examine why.

Busting the Fear of the Zeroes

That extra zero on the profit creates what I call *"the fear of the zeroes."* People think high ticket deals are too complex, or they won't understand it. But here's what I can tell you from personal experience, the process of flipping a $50,000 junker house to someone looking to buy a $50,000 junker house is the same process as flipping an $11,000,000 apartment complex to someone looking to buy an $11,000,000 apartment complex. It's just different buyer profiles.

Once you understand that every deal is the same, you are free to start or move into larger deals, where there's 1) greater profit per transaction, 2) less emotion and 3) less competition. And again, that's why I recommend that you get started with *small* apartments for your first deal and then transition into mid-size and large apartments. Here's someone who busted the fear of the zeroes.

Case Study – Window Installer Makes $60,000 on First Deal

Peter Arianas was a window installer who lived in New York. This was his very first real estate deal of any kind other than owning his home. He found a property in Ohio, a 66-unit apartment building. He analyzed it sight unseen and put it under contract to purchase. He flipped his contract to an end buyer and made $60,000 on his first deal.

Let's examine the transaction. Peter never took title. He didn't have to get approved for financing as he wasn't the end buyer. He did this across state lines – he was in New York, the property was in Ohio. He received $36,000 cash at closing from his end-buyer. On top of that, he negotiated with his buyer to pay him another $30,000 after closing from the cash flow of the property. Peter earned passive income from a building he didn't even own.

That's $66,000 in gross income. Now, Peter had to initially deposit $5,000 in earnest money to secure his contract. So he simply raised that from some friends and paid them back – with a return - out of his proceeds from closing. He netted $60,000 on his very first transaction. Peter didn't graduate from houses. He just decided to start with apartments.

Bonus Resource
Interview: *Window Installer Makes $60,000 on First Deal*
www.BMSABook.com/60k

Case Study – House Flipper Quadruples Profits with Seven-Plex

Let's return to Delwin Marks, the house flipper for 10 years. Earlier, I shared the story of how he flipped a four-plex and made $11,000 on his first small apartment deal – double the profits of his typical house flip.

Delwin took his success on a four-plex and on his next deal, he found a seven-unit small apartment which he placed under contract to flip. On that flip, he made $23,000 – double what he made on wholesaling the four-plex. In just two back-to-back transactions, he made $34,000. With his house flipping business, he would have had to do at least seven flips for the same profit. Delwin decided to focus on the larger deals.

Let's sum this up.

Pay Your Rent or Mortgage for One Year with One Deal

What's the impact of wholesaling higher ticket deals? Well, you could pay your rent or mortgage for one year by wholesaling just one apartment deal per year on a part-time basis.

Delwin Marks made $11,000 on his first small apartment flip. You divide $11,000 by 12 months and that's the equivalent of $916 per month; $916 per month goes a long way towards paying your rent or mortgage over the next year. On his next deal, Delwin made $23,000, which is the equivalent of $1,916 per month over 12 months. Now, if you do like Peter and you net $60,000 on one deal, that'll pay your rent and mortgage for a much longer period of time.

Of course, wholesaling is active income. Let's look at how you can reap the benefits of passive income by buying and holding small apartments.

Key #6: Use Passive Income and Appreciation to Buy More Assets

Now we're at Key #6: using passive income and appreciation to buy more income-producing assets.

Interest Rates are at Unprecedented Lows

Economic conditions plus the stimulus actions of the Federal Reserve Bank have combined to give us record lows on interest rates. The cost of money for conventional financing and private financing have both gone down and consequently, financing is *cheaper than ever*. That means one thing for you: more money in your pocket. Cash flow per door has basically doubled.

Let me explain. Recall, income properties are valued based upon net operating income, or NOI:

$$NOI (\$/yr) = Revenue - Expenses$$

As I showed in Key #3, apartments are hot because rental demand is high. That means rents and occupancies have increased, all contributing to increased revenues and increased NOI for apartments, which has beneficial impact on both cash flow and equity.

Cash Flow

Cash flow, the money in your pocket, is the difference between NOI and your mortgage payments, otherwise known as the Debt Service Payments:

$$Cash\ Flow (\$/yr) = NOI - Debt\ Service\ Payments$$

Thus, increased rental demand and decreased financing costs (conventional and private money) have contributed to greater cash flow per door (which is good). In a moment, I'll show how you'll use that to amass wealth. Before that, let's look at the second impact area from increased rental demand: increased equity.

Since apartments are valued and appraised based on the NOI, the value of a property goes up as the NOI goes up. So we can *force* the value of an apartment building to increase by raising rents and/or raising the occupancy. It's called Forced Appreciation and will be shown in detail in Chapter 5.

Forced Appreciation

Forced appreciation is different than market appreciation. Forced appreciation is something we can directly and measurably impact. Market appreciation is property value appreciation by outside market forces. It's a great bonus when it happens but not something we have control over. We control forced appreciation and that *predictability* is another reason I started with apartments.

Let me show you what I mean. I'll save the math for Chapter 5 (don't worry, it's simple math that a 6th grader can understand).

If you raise rent just $10 per month per unit for an apartment building, you raise the NOI and that raises the value of that property by $1,200 *per unit*. Do it for 10 units and you create $12,000 in equity. Do it for 50 units and it's $60,000. Do it for 100 units and it's $120,000, etc. See what I mean? And that's just a $10 increase. Raise it $20 and you get double the result.

Now that's just one way to increase the NOI and hence the value and equity of your property. You could also raise occupancy to raise NOI. A 2% occupancy increase in the building is also a $1,200 *per unit* value increase. Ten units means $12,000; 50 units means $60,000; 100 units means $120,000! A 2% occupancy increase on a 50 unit building is just 1 more unit continually leased.

Raise the rent $10 and raise the occupancy 2% at the same time and you double the results I've shown. It's an additive effect. That's the power of forced appreciation and that is how you create wealth in apartments. You take an underperforming property, make improvements, raise the rent, raise occupancy, and create a return on equity.

Nobody decides to move out because of a $10 rent increase. Even by just raising the rent or raising occupancy, you can double or triple your return on investment.

Use Cash Flow and Forced Appreciation to Amass Wealth

So back to Key #6, what can you do with that increased cash flow and increased equity in your apartment building?

Well, you could live off of the cash flow and pay less income tax than you would on active income, such as the income from a job. Or you could accumulate that cash flow into a fund to be used as the down payment on a larger apartment building and repeat the process but with more units, leading to more zeroes. *The fastest path to wealth creation is to create assets which produce income to purchase more income-producing assets.*

So how could you use your equity that was simultaneously created from forced appreciation? You could sell the property at the higher price and pull the cash out. Of course, you'll have a long term capital gains tax obligation on the increased equity portion.

Want to avoid the tax liability? Then you can take advantage of a special provision in the IRS Code, called Section 1031 and do a *1031 Exchange*. The IRS allows you to take your profits from the sale of real estate, and when you use it to purchase another piece of real estate within 6 months, there is ZERO tax due. That's right... ZERO. You can do this as many times as you want to amass wealth and you can even pass the benefit on to your heirs. It's fabulous. See a professional 1031 Exchange Intermediary on the details but it's done routinely.

But what if you don't want to sell your cash flowing property? Here's another way to leverage your equity but not sell your property. You refinance the property at the new higher value and pull your equity out as cash tax-free (loans are not taxable). You could then use that cash as the down payment on another larger property. Again, you can keep repeating the process, moving up to larger apartments each time, and adding extra zeroes to your deals and your profits.

The thing about forced appreciation, though, is that it *only exists in commercial* deals (5+ units), not residential deals such as houses and 2-4 units. With residential properties, appreciation is limited to market appreciation, which we can't control. And in the bad economy, there was no market appreciation. Zilch. Commercial deals are not dependent on this. We control the forced appreciation.

Now let's look at doing it all with none of your own cash.

Key #7: Use Other People's Money

Now that you understand the power of leveraging increased rents and equity thru forced appreciation and market appreciation, let me show how you get leverage-on-leverage by doing it all using other people's money.

Stock Market Meltdown Destroyed Confidence in the Market

The stock market losses of the past few years have changed the way money is invested. Yes, the markets have rebounded but the way this generation of investors view the market has changed – perhaps permanently. *And change creates opportunity for entrepreneurs.*

Massive amounts of money were pulled out of the markets and many investors, particularly older people – namely the huge population of Baby Boomers – have been incredibly reluctant to put it back in a risky and volatile market. The tens of millions of

Baby Boomers approaching – or already in – their retirement years cannot afford to gamble their retirement savings – their lives literally depend on it.

So there is a massive pool of money waiting to be invested in safer, less volatile alternatives to stocks. Real estate is one of those alternatives and this demographic of people are all over it. For example, in the United States today, there is $5 Trillion in investment retirement accounts (IRA's). And 97% of that money is earning less than 1% because it is sitting in cash, money markets or CD's – earning practically nothing. All because those investors don't want to go back into the stock market. And a portion of those investors are *self-directed IRA* holders who can individually choose what to invest in, such as your real estate deal. In Chapter 7, I'll explain how you can get your deals in front of this money.

It's money where there are no loan origination fees, no bank qualifying, and you negotiate the finance rate. There's no credit limit based on how many loans you have outstanding or even your credit score. It's all based on the security provided by the transaction and how it's structured to protect the investor. It's done privately and fully sanctioned by the IRS.

Another advantage of small apartments is that not a lot of cash is required to buy them. You find just one self-directed IRA holder with $50,000 to a few hundred thousand dollars and you have a bank. You can easily do your first deal. And from there, you expand your private money sources – if nothing else, from the referrals of your first investor.

And that's just *one source* of private funding. How many more deals could you do and how fast could you build your portfolio if you were not limited by your cash or credit? And if you want to know a simple truth, it's generally simpler to raise big money than it is small money.

Case Study – Two Unemployed Partners Raise $6 Million

Denon Williams and Terry Warren are my $6 Million Men. When I met them, they had zero real estate experience besides owning their own homes. They had been laid off from their respective jobs of 25 years and wanted to use the opportunity to start buying income-producing real estate, all in order to break their dependency on an employer.

Their problem was that since they were laid-off, they had no W-2 income to show and they couldn't get a traditional loan from a bank. They were "unbankable" while also in the midst of the greatest credit meltdown since the Great Depression. They decided to use other people's money instead, and funded $6 million across four real estate transactions over the next ten months. They did it all using none of their own cash, none of their own credit, and with no prior experience in real estate.

Bonus Resource
Interview: *Circle of Champions Roundtable Interview*
www.BMSABook.com/roundtable

How is that possible? They used my Raising Private Money Formula.

Raising Private Money Formula

I will cover this in detail in Chapter 7 but as way of an introduction, here are the four parts of the Raising Private Money Formula to finding and structuring private money deals in real estate:

- **Part 1**: Predisposed
- **Part 2**: Control
- **Part 3**: Low risk
- **Part 4**: High return

Part 1: Predisposed

When it comes time to seek funding sources for your project, focus on **Predisposed** sources: investors, people, or groups that are looking to invest in real estate. They already believe in real estate as an asset class; they don't need to be sold on the merits of real estate. They just need to understand your deal. Two examples of predisposed sources which I've already introduced are sellers (thru owner financing) and self-directed IRA investors – other people's IRA (OPI). I'll introduce more sources in Chapter 7.

Bonus Resource
Webinar: *How to Invest in Real Estate Using IRA's*
www.BMSABook.com/ira

Once you've identified the predisposed sources, the rest of the formula is about structuring your deal so that it is attractive to the investor. Your investment has to be both appealing and low-risk and the rest of the formula structures the deal such that it speaks to the psychology of the private lender.

Here's the key: the investor needs to feel confident they will get their principal back before they hear about their return. As an IRA investor once said, *"Tell me about return OF my capital before you tell me about return ON my capital."* That is what the next three parts of the formula accomplish.

Part 2: Control

Part 2 of the formula is **Control**. Structure the transaction so that it provides the investor a feeling of control. This is paramount. We want them to feel that if they invest their money in our project and the terms of the arrangement are not satisfied, they can take control and get their money out.

Control is one of the strongest feelings that humans crave, especially in the wake of the 2008-2009 stock market melt-down when investors felt like they had no control. An example of control is providing the ability for the investor to change the management company or change the manager of the LLC or take back the property, in the event of non-performance.

Part 3: Low Risk

Part 3 of the formula is **Low Risk**. Once the investor has that feeling of control, they now need to feel they won't have to exercise control since this is a low risk investment for them. So in this part of the formula, you systematically identify all of the risk elements of the project and design strategies for mitigating that risk. An example of a risk mitigating strategy is purchasing business income loss insurance to replace lost rent revenue in the event a portion of the property were to burn.

Show them how you have proactively acted in *their* interests to protect their money. Even if you have no experience (like Denon Williams and Terry Warren, or anyone doing a first deal), this is how you develop credibility with your investor through your preparation. They see you have their interests in mind. And you have answered the first part of their silent thinking, *"Tell me about return OF my capital..."*

Once that's done (and not before), you can now discuss *"return ON their capital,"* which leads to the last part of the formula.

Part 4: High Return

The last part, **High Return**, is about giving them a high return *relative to the low risk* you created. Now, this doesn't mean you just go wave some huge return to private investors and scare them away. That is what amateurs do, and that's why they don't fund deals.

Just as in any investment, the lower the perceived risk, the lower the expected return. So you first structure the deal so that you can present one with Control and Low Risk. And as you consistently demonstrate and make the case that the project is low risk, not only do you *establish your credibility* but the investor's expectations of the financial return are simultaneously *lowered*.

So, as the final step, and because everyone wants a "deal," you are going to satisfy that desire by providing the investor a return that is just above their (low return) expectations; expectations which you justifiably created in your structuring of the transaction to protect their interests. You give them a little more than they expect. And that's how to raise any amount for real estate, whether $5,000 or $5 million.

Use this Raising Private Money Formula to begin creating and expanding your real estate empire. In the process, you will find you are able to attract more investors by your focus on Control and Low Risk while not having to "give away the farm" for private money – which means more of the financial benefit stays with you, and you enjoy more repeat investors. With this formula, you can play bigger.

Bonus Resource
Webinar: *How to Raise Huge Money in Today's Economy*
www.BMSABooks.com/rpm

Recap: Advantages of Small Apartments

Now that you know the *7 Keys to Building a Real Estate Empire*, let's bring it back and summarize for you, Why Small Apartments?

- Rental demand is up
- LOTS of small apartments for deal flow
- Little competition
- Small apartments close fast
- Hedge funds don't pursue small and mid-size apartments
- Can quick-flip apartments just like houses
- LOTS of Buyers for small apartment flips
- Big wholesale fees
- Little cash to raise for purchase
- Able to hire management companies
- Can combine small apartments with your house business
- Can scale-up to larger deals
- Can increase property values thru forced appreciation

- Make offers sight unseen from your kitchen table
- No driving for dollars
- No Dodd-Frank restrictions (if not owner-occupied)
- No prior experience needed

For all of the reasons above, I chose to start with small apartments and that's why you can too.

Coming Up...

In the next chapter, you are going to learn why the competition is so low in multifamily. I'll go ahead and tell you it's due to three *limiting beliefs* (or false myths) that I'm going to quickly dispel so you'll realize that you are qualified to start right now in multifamily and bypass the competition in single family.

Chapter Summary

- Small apartments are 2-30 units. There are LOTS of small apartments.
- Apartments are the perfect real estate niche that provides you greater leverage with *less competition*. They are IDEAL.
- Hedge funds don't pursue small or mid-size apartments.
- You can quick-flip a small apartment like a house to get your critical first deal.
- There are lots of buyers for small apartment flips, particularly burned-out single family landlords and small business owners.
- Pursue High Ticket deals (like apartments) rather than High Volume deals (like houses). There's greater leverage of your time and less competition.
- When wholesaling, it's reasonable to expect to make $10,000+ per small apartment contract flip vs. $2,000-$5,000 for a house contract flip.
- You can pay your rent or mortgage for one year by wholesaling one apartment contract per year.

- You can scale-up from small apartments to mid-size and large apartments.
- You are qualified to start with small apartments; you don't need to graduate from single-family.
- Apartments may be wholesaled or held for passive income.
- Apartments are built to cash flow; houses are built to be sold to homeowners.
- The cost of money is at lifetime lows so cash flow per door is at lifetime highs.
- Flipping houses is like starting from scratch every time, and that's no way to build an empire.
- No matter how much money you have, you will run out and you should use OPM to get leverage in your wealth accumulation.
- The largest private investing group for small apartments is self-directed IRA holders.
- The *7 Keys to Building a Real Estate Empire* can help individuals reach a maximum level of success.

7 Keys to Building a Real Estate Empire

- **Key #1: Marketing, Marketing, Marketing** - You are in the marketing business. You are always marketing for two things: *deals and dollars.* On properties you own, you also market for *residents.*
- **Key #2: Close Your First Deal** - Your most critical deal is your first deal.
- **Key #3: Pick a Niche in Demand** – Feed the "starving crowd." Apartment rental demand is up nationwide. It's a HOT niche.
- **Key #4: Leverage Every Activity** - Everything in real estate is about leverage; leverage of your time, your effort, other people's money, etc.

- **Key #5: Do Larger and Larger Deals** – The paydays are bigger and the competition is less when you shift to a "High Ticket" business. Bust the fear of the zeroes.

- **Key #6: Use Passive Income and Appreciation to Buy More Assets** - You can predictably and rapidly expand your wealth growth with commercial properties. It's called "Forced Appreciation."

- **Key #7: Use Other People's Money** – Get leverage upon leverage by combining the Raising Private Money Formula with *forced appreciation*.

Bonus Resources Summary

Interview: *Circle of Champions Roundtable Interview*
www.BMSABook.com/roundtable

Interview: *House Flipper Doubles Profits with Four-Plex*
www.BMSABook.com/double

Interview: *Window Installer Makes $60,000 on First Deal*
www.BMSABook.com/60k

Interview: *$24,000 from Her First Small Apartment Flip*
www.BMSABook.com/triplexes

Webinar: *7 Keys to Building a Real Estate Empire*
www.BMSABook.com/7keys

Webinar: *How to Invest in Real Estate Using IRA's*
www.BMSABook.com/ira

Webinar: *How to Raise Huge Money in Today's Economy*
www.BMSABooks.com/rpm

Webinar: *Real Estate Tax Strategies Your CPA Doesn't Know*
www.BMSABook.com/taxes

Chapter 3

Why is the Competition So Low?

M
y mentor pushed me to begin with apartments for all of the advantages I cited in the previous chapter. So with that being the case, why are there always so few players in the multifamily space? There's lots of people in single family, why are there so few in multifamily?

Well, I'll tell you right now there are three prevalent, limiting beliefs - or myths - that are keeping people out of this space and they're false beliefs. And the sooner you understand them as being false, the sooner you come to realize this is your opportunity. Those three limiting beliefs, or myths, are:

- **Myth #1**: You have to graduate from single family to multifamily
- **Myth #2**: You need big cash and credit to buy apartments
- **Myth #3**: You have to deal with tenants and toilets

These are all FALSE but I need to show you why so you realize that right now – no matter your background or experience - you are qualified to start with apartments. Once you realize that, your mind will be prepared to learn how to do it. So in this chapter, I am *myth busting*.

Busting Myth #1: Graduating from Houses

Let me begin with a story.

10 Units vs. 10 Houses

I was at a Saturday real estate club years ago and as I was greeting people, an experienced colleague approached me. He was very experienced in houses; he bought houses, he flipped houses, he even taught people how to do houses. In the conversation, he said to me, *"Lance, my goal is to acquire 10 rental houses over the next 12 months."*

Now, in my silence, I couldn't imagine a more tortuous endeavor. First to buy 10 houses would mean looking at probably 100 deals, then negotiating 10 deals with 10 different owners. And if you did it, you'd have to oversee 10 properties scattered all over the city. Ugh. So I replied to him, *"Instead of buying 10 houses, have you considered buying two five-plexes or one 10-unit apartment?"* His reply shocked me.

Here was a person very experienced with houses. He said, *"Maybe someday I'll graduate to apartments."* And that demonstrated to me the importance of mindset in getting started in this business and the false notion that somehow there was a graduation process. Not only was his strategy flawed but he would spend far more time and money acquiring 10 houses than 10 apartment units and he'd end up with far less cash flow.

It's important to understand that there is no necessity of graduating from single family to multifamily. There is no graduation process. Rather, I recommend *beginning with multifamily* for all the reasons cited in Chapter 2. If you're already doing houses, add apartments now.

Somehow, people have the notion that they need to first do some house deals and then after they've done a sufficient, yet unspecified, number of house deals, they will attend a cap and gown ceremony where they walk across a stage and someone will certify them as qualified to begin with apartments. If you're looking for that certification, congratulations; you are certified.

Seriously, my students across the country are beginning with multifamily units by using the techniques outlined in this book. I've shown and will continue to show Case Studies of students from all backgrounds who, as first-time apartment entrepreneurs, flipped or purchased multifamily properties as their very first real estate deal. Most started with larger apartment properties than even my first deal.

The real issue is obtaining the knowledge and mindset – the purpose of this book.

Case Study – My First Offer Earns Me 100% Financing

My first investment property was a four-plex. I bought it 100% seller financed, which means I used none of my own cash; the seller received monthly mortgage payments from me. As a result, I had nothing-down cash flow at Day 1. The seller lived in Hawaii and as I was leaving the closing, I called her up and said, "*Ms. Mansson, the property is sold.*" And she said, "*Thank you, Mr. Edwards. Thank you.*"

That was an "Aha Moment" for me. On my first deal, as an absolutely green newbie, I bought this property at 85 cents on the dollar with 100% financing over 30 years, and no balloon payment. I got a good deal and Ms. Mansson got what she wanted. It was at that point, that my Little Voice finally admitted, "*My gosh, we really can do this.*"

So the whole point I want to share with you again – I'm going to keep reinforcing it throughout the training – is that you do not have to graduate from single family to multifamily. You're qualified *right now* to get started in apartments.

All right, that was limiting belief #1. Let's look at the second limiting belief that holds people back and stops them unnecessarily from getting started in apartments.

Busting Myth #2: Need Cash or Credit

There's this lingering question: *"Don't I need big cash or credit to do apartments?"* And this is a big one for people. It's a logical question. Apartments are higher ticket items and newbies naturally believe they need to use their own financial resources to do these deals, as if they were qualifying to buy a home. Well, it's a false belief and to make this point I'm going to begin by pointing out your role in real estate. And in the process, I'm going to have to speak some real estate *blasphemy*.

Investor vs. Entrepreneur

Let's look at the language we use and how we are labeled. In our industry we are called what? Real estate what? Real estate *investors*, right? I am a member of a real estate *investing* association and you should be too. They are great organizations.

But when I say the term *"investor,"* what connotation comes to mind? What does an investor have a lot of? That's right, an investor has *cash, capital or money*. Well, wait a minute. As a newbie, I'm being told I'm a real estate *investor* but I'm told to go out and do these nothing-down deals.

And what happens oftentimes is many beginning real estate investors - who have limited assets at their disposal – are out declaring themselves a real estate investor but in the back of their mind, there's a little voice that's saying, *"Hey, wait a minute, you don't have the cash to buy these properties. You don't even have the credit. How are you going to buy anything – you're not really a real estate investor."*

And that nagging little voice is enough to shut people down because we will not take any action which is not congruent with our identity about who we are. We're just wired that way. And so by labeling ourselves as real estate *investors*, we are actually doing more harm than good.

Now, on the other hand, let's look at the label *entrepreneur*. What does an entrepreneur look for? An entrepreneur looks for *deals, and opportunities*. We are *deal makers*.

Look at the definition of an entrepreneur: *an entrepreneur is someone who pursues his or her vision using the time, talent and resources (i.e. cash and credit) of others*. And the key word here is *others*.

So when you look at that definition and what our job is, you see that we are not real estate investors, we are real estate *entrepreneurs*. As entrepreneurs, our job is to go out and market to find the deals and market to find the dollars, and we match make. We marry deals and dollars together and that's how we create value and that's how we generate our profits. We are matchmakers.

Change Your Label

So if your business card says your name and the title "Real Estate Investor" and your intent is to go out and put together deals using other people's money, I urge you to change your business cards. Throw away that box of cards and get a new deck that says your name with the title *"Real Estate Entrepreneur"* - because that's your role in the process.

When you declare yourself as an *entrepreneur*, people understand it's not going to be your money. And more importantly, your little voice understands that it's not about your money or credit. Now your label for yourself is congruent with your identity. Entrepreneurs bring the deals to the dollars. Investors bring the dollars to the deals. The key is they have to be *solid* apartment deals. I'll show you how to evaluate them in Chapter 5.

So, as an entrepreneur, getting involved with apartments is not about your personal financial resources; it's about your ability to market and match-make deals and dollars. Once you understand this role, you quickly realize that it's not about your cash or credit.

Now, on to the third and final limiting belief...

Busting Myth #3: Dealing with Tenants and Toilets

I've demonstrated the power of passive income and forced appreciation from buying and holding - while revealing your role as the entrepreneur, rather than the investor. I've introduced the Raising Private Money Formula but there's a third limiting belief that is holding people back falsely and that is this: *"Well, don't I have to deal with tenants and toilets? I don't want to deal with tenants and toilets."*

Do you think I want to deal with tenants and toilets? No, I wouldn't be in this business if I had to deal with tenants and toilets. And so how do you avoid dealing with tenants and toilets? You already know the answer. You're going to use property management companies. But, let's talk about management companies in the context of *small apartments*. First, let's set a baseline of property management for *large* apartments.

Case Study – Foreign Buyer Creates Stellar Investment Opportunity

We did an $11 Million, 294 unit project in Houston, Texas where the buyer was from Canada. He was purchasing the property for long-term passive income. And since he was 2,500 miles away, it wasn't going to be possible for him to drive by his property every Saturday afternoon and check on it (obviously). So we found him a management company. And the key word here is *company* – a management company that has *staff*, *processes* and *systems* for management of multifamily properties.

They do everything. They manage the property, they do the leasing, they do the maintenance, they pay the bills, and they send him the checks.

Management Companies

And that is what you want with your small apartments. So, when I say property management, I mean a *company*; not an individual person - not a realtor who does property management on the side. I've already introduced the importance of systems in any business so you want a management company with *systems*, comprised of *people, processes* and *technology*. If one person gets sick, the property management doesn't come to a screeching halt.

You are going to use a management company which specializes in small apartments. They manage several hundred units for multiple owners. Not only will they have systems but you can leverage their economies of scale. Let's look at that.

Economies of Scale

Here's three ways you'll leverage the scale of your property management company:

- **Scale #1**: Roving maintenance team
- **Scale #2**: Buying power
- **Scale #3**: Experience when raising private money

Scale #1: Roving Maintenance Team

First, you are going to leverage their maintenance team to reduce your costs of maintenance. Now, a large 294 unit property like the one described above has its own full-time maintenance team on-site. They'll have a certified air conditioning tech and 1-2 other maintenance men who can handle 95% of the daily maintenance, at cost. They are paid an hourly rate – much less than the cost of calling in an independent contractor who has trip fees and profit embedded in his fees.

A large property can afford to have on-site staff but if you own a four-plex or a 10 unit or even a 20 unit building, you can't afford an on-site maintenance staff. It's cost prohibitive because you don't have the economy of scale like a large property. But your management company does have that economy of scale by the fact it manages hundreds of units for individual owners.

Your management company will have a *roving* maintenance team comprised of certified maintenance techs. They rove from property to property handling the daily repair and maintenance tasks of the management company's clients. When our property has a repair need, the roving crew is assigned by the management company and the property is billed just for the hours associated with the work. And because the crew is on the payroll of the management company at an hourly rate, you get the work done at cost, saving you on expenses.

Scale #2: Buying Power

Another way you'll leverage your management company is through their *buying power*. A company that has purchase authority for several hundred units has buying power with the suppliers and vendors who service your apartment building. For example, the management company will have deeper discounts in buying rehab and maintenance materials than you can have as a single small apartment owner. And so you get supplies at the management company's costs – further saving your expenses.

Case Study – Insurance Savings Pay the Management Fee

I had a management company one time which managed my properties and 2,000 other doors for other owners. All they did was apartment management. Based on their buying power, they were able to negotiate a master insurance policy for the benefit of all their owner clients. I could elect to include my properties as a rider under that master insurance policy, along with the other owners. Under their policy, the savings from my insurance premium were GREATER than the cost of my management fee – which made it a no-brainer.

What's another way you can leverage the management company?

Scale #3: Experience When Raising Private Money

A fairly common question I receive from newbies is, *"How can I raise private money on an apartment when I have no prior experience?"* It's a good question and I want to answer it here.

First, you do it by using the Raising Private Money Formula which I introduced in the previous chapter and will cover in detail in Chapter 7. When you structure your deal properly, you are positioning yourself credibly with the investor.

Second, the investor doesn't care about your experience. What they really care about is how much *risk* there is for *their* investment. Any question about your experience has little to do with you and EVERYTHING to do with the investor. They are assessing risk. So how do you mitigate that risk if you don't have experience? After all, management company experience is an important attribute of any investment. What do you do?

Remember, you're an entrepreneur. Your job is to utilize the time, talent and resources of *others*. So, you *leverage* the experience of your management company. You use your management company's resume when putting together your Project Packet to present to investors or a bank. Find and utilize a management company with a killer resume and say, *"Here's my team. That's our experience."*

Bonus Resource
Webinar: *How to Present to Private Money Investors*
www.BMSABook.com/present

Those are the 3 main leverage points afforded by management companies. And the best part, the property pays their fee.

The Property Pays the Management Fee

Now, I don't know if you've had any experience with managing single family homes. I've had a few, and only a few, because it is very difficult to find managers, good property managers who are really going to take care of your property. Why is that? Because there is not enough money in it for them.

I don't know why anyone would do it. The idea of going house to house, driving all over the city to chase down random checks and do this and do that for 8% or 10% of the collections on a house is really not worth it.

And so it is very difficult to find good property managers to manage *houses*. But when you have a small apartment with *multiple* units in *one location*, there is an efficiency of management there. When you have a mid-size property, you can even afford to have an on-site manager. Even in small apartments, you can cut a small rent break to a resident to keep an eye on the property 24/7 and show units, collect rents, etc.

So that's *another reason* why investors select multifamily over single family – because you can afford to hire better management companies and pay them enough so they are able to do the job right.

Asset Management vs. Property Management

And so the rule that I always share with my students is this: *never, never, never self-manage*. You manage the managers. Your role is *Asset Management*, not property management.

You choose and hire the property management company. They are responsible for the daily operation and reporting to you. You keep tab on their performance thru your weekly and monthly Performance Reports. It's just like any business.

Bonus Resource
Webinar: *How to Make Big Money in Small Apartments*
www.BMSABook.com/bmsa

Coming Up...

In the next chapter, you are going to learn how to replace the "40 Year Plan for Retirement" we were taught in school with the "Five Year Plan for Retirement." It's all possible with small apartments and can be done using none of your own cash or credit.

Chapter Summary

- Competition is low in apartments because of three limiting beliefs (or myths). The three facts are:
  - ✓ **Fact #1**: You don't need to graduate from single family to multifamily. You can start with multifamily like I did and my students do.
  - ✓ **Fact #2**: You don't need to use your own cash or credit to buy apartments.
  - ✓ **Fact #3**: You don't have to deal with tenants and toilets.
- You are qualified right now to do apartments. If you are a newbie, start with apartments. If you are doing houses now, add apartments.
- If you intend to put together deals using OPM, you are a Real Estate *Entrepreneur*; NOT a Real Estate *Investor*. As such, this business has nothing to do with the amount of your personal resources.
- An entrepreneur is someone who pursues his or her vision using the time, talents and resources (i.e. cash or credit) of *others*.
- Again, you are in the marketing business. You market for *deals and dollars*.

- Hire management *companies* which already manage hundreds of apartment doors. Leverage their scale and experience in three ways:
    1. Roving maintenance team
    2. Buying power
    3. Experience when raising private money
- Another advantage of multifamily is you can afford to hire good management *companies*.
- Never self-manage. Be an Asset Manager NOT a Property Manager. Manage the managers.

Bonus Resources Summary

Webinar: *How to Present to Private Money Investors*
www.BMSABook.com/present

Webinar: *How to Make Big Money in Small Apartments*
www.BMSABook.com/bmsa

Chapter 4

The Free in Five Plan

I've made the case for why you should get started with small apartments and why you are qualified right now. I've shown that it's not about your own cash or credit but rather your ability to match-make deals and dollars.

With that background, now let me show you how you are going to use small apartments to become financially free within five years. When I learned this, it changed everything for me.

To begin, I need to review the three components of wealth creation and financial freedom generation.

Three Components of Wealth Creation

All three components of wealth creation are available to you simultaneously with apartments:

1. Active income
2. Passive income
3. Net worth

Let's quickly define them.

Active Income

I assume you're probably clear about active income. That's where you trade your time for dollars and you understand this really, really well. In fact, too well because we've all had a lifetime of being trained on how to be good employees. So I'm sure you get this. It's a job. You understand active income.

What's another type of active income besides a job? Well, wholesaling. If you're out wholesaling apartments like the Case Studies in this book, it's active income. You get paid for your active involvement. It pays very well but, nevertheless, you have to stay active in order to have the checks coming in.

Passive Income

So the second component of financial freedom is passive income. Now, passive income is your *mailbox money*. That's where you get paid whether you're actively involved or not. You might be active up-front setting it in motion but once it's there, it keeps coming passively. And in the case of apartments, it's from rental income. Apartments were *created* to be passive income vehicles.

Net Worth

Now the third component is net worth. Net worth is your savings, your nest egg, it's your accumulated assets. It's your retirement plan, your 401K. In the case of apartments, it's the equity in your buildings – which you can grow thru forced appreciation and/or market appreciation.

Those are the three components of wealth creation and all three have a role and, again, all three are possible with apartments. But financial freedom is all about *passive income*.

Now, before I show you the Five Year Plan to financial freedom, let me review with you the model we were taught in school. At least, this is the one I was taught in school and I bet it's the same one you learned as well.

Old School – 40 Year Financial Freedom Plan

The model that I was taught in school about generating financial independence was taught to me when I was very young. I think in the first grade they pulled me aside and told me this, *"Little Lance, here is how you're going to generate financial independence for yourself. You're going to come here for the next twelve years and you're going to work hard, study hard and get good grades. And then, Little Lance, after twelve years you're going to graduate from high school."*

"From there, you take your good grades so you can get accepted to a good college. And while there, Little Lance, we want you to work hard, study hard and get good grades for four, six or eight more years. And then when you come out of college, we want you to take your good grades and go out and get a good job."

Everything sound familiar so far? They didn't stop there.

They continued, *"Then with that good job, we want you to work hard for the next 40 years earning active income. And we want you to save a portion of your active income from every paycheck over the next 40 years and build up your net worth through your 401K or retirement plan."*

"Finally, after 40 years, and once you've accumulated a sufficiently large net worth and nest egg, you're then going to retire by converting that nest egg into passive income and live off that passive income for whatever remaining years you may have."

Sound painfully familiar? Did they teach this at your school? I call it the *40 Year Plan*.

Now, the 40 Year Plan can work provided that you are saving a *lot* of your active income in the *early years* and you can enjoy the benefits of compound interest working for you.

If you start late or if you experience an equity market meltdown like we had in late 2008, you find that all of a sudden you can't make it. You don't have enough time left to accumulate a net worth sufficient to retire and have enough passive income. And that model has left many people stranded right now; this whole notion that you have to have a large net worth in order to have financial independence.

So the model that I want to share with you is a different model. This model is still based on the fact that *financial freedom is about passive income*.

Our Financial Freedom Definition

Our definition of financial freedom is different than the one taught in school.

DEFINITION: *Financial freedom is when you earn more than enough passive income to pay for your desired lifestyle.*

Now if you examine that definition, you'll notice it says nothing about your net worth. It says nothing about how much you have in your 401K. It says nothing about how much you have in the bank. What it does talk about is *having enough passive income to pay for your desired lifestyle*.

So how do you apply this? If your desired lifestyle costs $5,000 per month, then by definition, the moment you have at least $5,000 per month passive income, you're financially free. You've got enough passive income to pay the bills and you're free to go fire your boss and either go generate more passive income or you're then free to go build your net worth.

So if passive income is your objective, how do you become financially free in five years, using none of your own cash or credit? Let me show you our "Free in Five Plan."

New School – Five Year Financial Freedom Plan

Let's say your desired lifestyle costs $5,000 per month and your objective is to be financially free within five years, which is a very conservative timeframe by the way. So the question is, how do you receive $5,000 per month passive income within five years? Here's your Five Year Plan.

In Year 1 of the Five Year Plan, you have *one* objective. That one objective is to acquire one small apartment that generates $1,000 a month cash flow. You've got one year to do it. Just find one. So at the end of Year 1, you're getting $1,000 a month passive income. (I've already shown you how you are going to fund it and I'll show you more in Chapter 7 so remove that limitation from your head).

Now in Year 2, here's what I want you to do. *Go do it again*. Find a second small apartment that generates another $1,000 per month cash flow and acquire it. So at the end of Year 2 you own two small apartments, generating a combined $2,000 a month.

I think you see where I'm going with this. In Year 3, you find a third property, at $1,000 a month, Year 4, the same, Year 5, the same. By the end of Year 5, you have five small apartments - each throwing off $1,000 a month cash flow. In total, you have $5,000 per month cash flow and - by definition - you're financially free.

At that point, you have choices. You're free to do more of the same to continue to increase your passive income. You're free to fire your boss and don't do anything with regards to generating more active income. And/or you're free to then go build your net worth.

Bonus Resource
Webinar: *How to Make Big Money in Small Apartments*
www.BMSABook.com/bmsa

Turning the Old School Model Upside Down

Here's the thing... We were taught in school to take forty years working for someone else to build up our *net worth* and then live off the passive income. We're turning that model upside down.

What I am urging you to do is take the next three to five years to focus on first building up your *passive income*. Then, once you are financially free, take the *rest of your life* building up your net worth but do it on *your time* and *your terms*. Recall, you could build up your net worth simply by growing the equity in your apartment buildings.

You see, it is far faster and easier to become financially free than it is to become wealthy. Wealth can take decades; financial freedom can be accomplished in a few short years.

Flip 1, Flip 1, Flip 1, Hold 1

And along the way to financial freedom and accumulating apartments, you can generate chunks of cash to pay today's bills by wholesaling apartments. I believe you should *"Always Be Wholesaling."* If you are creating deal flow, you want to monetize every lead possible.

In the process of creating deal flow, you will come across deals which are too small, too ugly, too much work, etc. They may not meet *your* buying criteria but they meet *someone else's* criteria. Place them under contract and flip them. So your model becomes, *flip 1, flip 1, flip 1, hold 1*. Cherry pick the deals you want to hang on to and flip the others for chunks of cash.

That is your Five Year Plan to financial freedom. And it's five years only if you're lazy. It can be much faster than that once you understand how to find the deals and how to do it using other people's money because then there's no limit to how fast you can get there. So let's set your target.

How to Determine Your Number

What's important is for you to determine your "number." Instead of focusing on how much net worth you need to have 40 years from now, it's more important to determine how much passive income you need *today* in order to be financially free. Start with how much you need per month to pay your bills. Let's say it's $8,300 per month, or $100,000 per year.

You then translate that target into the *number of apartment doors* you need to own or control. Here are the ratios:

# of Apartment Doors	Cash Flow ($ / Year)
160	$200,000
80	$100,000
40	$50,000

So if you come to me and you say, "Lance, I need $100,000 a year cash flow to live my desired lifestyle," I'm going to tell you that's 80 apartment doors that you need to own or control. If you need half that income, use half the number of doors. If you need double that, double the number of doors. It's all scalable.

If you do the math it comes out to roughly $100 a month cash flow per apartment unit, not apartment complex, but per apartment *unit*.

Let's say your target is $100,000 a year and 80 units. Do you have to buy one 80-unit apartment building? You can; but if you want to spread it out over five years, that's 16 units per year. Could you do that? You could even start with five units and grow from there.

The reason for my emphasis on small apartments is that I believe that's the best place to get started. Start small and then expand from there but get that critical first deal done, quickly.

I'm showing you that you're closer to financial freedom than you ever realized. You're as close as your number of doors target. We've been taught to think of retirement as something that happens in our 60's. It can happen three to five years from now once you understand the proper model to get there.

And so the question I'm posing to you is how many units do you need to declare your financial freedom? Don't worry about where the money's coming from because I'm going to show you how to do that in Chapter 7. But if you had access to the funding sources and you knew how to find the deals, *how many apartment units do you need to declare your financial freedom* because that's the number I want you to focus on, that short-term objective.

Case Study – 12-Unit Property Yields $3,500 per Month

Denon Williams and Terry Warren are the two business partners who had been laid off when I first met them. They had no prior real estate experience and wanted to buy income producing real estate but were unbankable; thanks to no longer having any W-2 income to show. Despite that, they bought a 12-unit apartment in North Carolina that was an immense cash cow. This 12-unit bread-and-butter small apartment produced $3,500 per month cash flow, or nearly $300 per unit. That's *three times* what I told you to expect per door.

They received that extra cash flow thanks to a strategy called "Buy Acres, Sell Lots" which you'll learn in Chapter 8. Basically, it's a strategy where you rent by the bedroom, rather than by the unit.

You may be asking, *"But what about the bank financing to purchase it?"* They didn't need it. They *asked* for and received owner financing from the seller. Denon and Terry bought this property with 100% financing and no bank qualifying. You'll learn more about how you will do this in Chapter 7.

Bonus Resource
Webinar: *How to Raise Huge Money in Today's Economy*
www.BMSABook.com/rpm

Now, let's take a look at another example of passive income where you don't even own the property.

Case Study – Seller Financing Creates $10,000 Passive Income

In Chapter 2, I explained how the use of owner financing is a way to quickly flip or sell small apartments. Owner financing is also a great way to generate passive income for you with apartments. You can be the bank and not even own the property.

Recall the 10-unit apartment I sold with owner-financing in 22 days to a single family landlord. I kept my original bank mortgage in place and sold the property on what's called a *"wrap-around mortgage"* where my buyer's mortgage to me *wrapped* around my existing mortgage to my bank.

Here are the numbers. My mortgage had a balance of $105,000 and a monthly payment of $1,600 to the bank. I quick-sold the 10 unit for $180,000; the buyer paid me $27,000 cash as down payment (15% down) and monthly payments of $2,400. So how does it work?

I receive $2,400 per month as their mortgage payment. Out of their $2,400 per month, I pay $1,600 per month to my underlying bank mortgage so I net $800 per month, or approximately $10,000 per year, passive income, on a property I don't even own. I also make sure they pay me the pro-rated property taxes and insurance with their mortgage payment so I know the funds are in escrow with me when the annual insurance and tax bills come due.

You might say, *"But wait a minute. What if they don't make a payment?"* I *hope* they miss a payment because if they do, I can foreclose, take the property back and get another $27,000 cash down payment from the next buyer.

With small apartments, you can do this over and over again. Ten small apartment deals like the one above yields $100,000 per year passive income and $270,000 cash down payments. You can even put together wholesale deals with yourself in the middle and *earn residual passive income checks on properties which you have never even owned.*

Coming Up...

In the next chapter, you are going to learn what you need in order to get started in small apartments and how you can analyze and do deals from your kitchen table, or office desk - sight unseen and nationwide.

Chapter Summary

- There are three components of wealth creation - all available thru small apartments:
    1. Active Income
    2. Passive Income
    3. Net Worth
- Definition: *Financial Freedom is when you earn more than enough passive income to pay for your desired lifestyle*
- Financial freedom is about *passive income*; NOT net worth (as we were taught in school with the "40 Year Plan")
- Five Year Plan: *Flip 1, Flip 1, Flip 1, Hold 1* – flip apartment contracts to pay your bills today. Cherry pick the ones to hold and build up your passive income portfolio.
- Small apartments can have you financially free in five years by just doing one deal per year (and using OPM).
- The NUMBER to focus on is the number of doors you need to own or control for passive income. Start small to get your first deal done and then scale-up.
- You are closer to financial freedom this moment than you probably realized.
- Owner financing is another powerful way to generate passive income for yourself.

Bonus Resources Summary

Webinar: *How to Make Big Money in Small Apartments*
www.BMSABook.com/bmsa

Webinar: *How to Raise Huge Money in Today's Economy*
www.BSMABook.com/rpm

Chapter 5

What You Need to Get Started

Everything up until now has been *why* you need to get started. So now, let's talk about *what* you need to get started? Here are the essentials, and I will bet anything that you already have these resources at your disposal:

- Phone
- Internet access
- Basic calculator
- Sixth grade math skills

That's it. And you don't need an automobile.

Real Estate vs. "Feel Estate"

Years ago, a commercial broker told me this, *"Apartments are real estate. Houses are feel-estate."* And what he meant by that has to do with how apartments are valued, in contrast to houses.

Houses are valued based on comparable prices and the amenities. So a house valuation is quite *subjective*, dependent on the kitchen and bathroom updates and market comps for the area. It's "feel estate;" a potential buyer has to "feel" like a house could be their home.

You aren't going to fall in love with your apartment buildings. Apartment valuations are driven by the financials, it's very *objective*.

Apartment Valuations Are Based on the Numbers

It's all based on the numbers. Apartments are classified as *income-producing* properties which means their valuation is based on their income, specifically their *net operating income*, or NOI.

There are two basic formulas that you need to understand to evaluate any apartment anywhere in the country (this applies to all commercial properties). The first formula is:

- NOI (\$/yr) = Revenue – Expenses

NOI is *net operating income*. Revenue is all income sources, primarily rents but also includes late fees, laundry income, vending machines, etc. Expenses are all of the normal costs to operate the property including management fees, taxes, insurance, repairs and maintenance and utilities, etc. However, expenses do NOT include the mortgage payments. That comes in a little later. The second equation is:

- Cap Rate (%) = NOI / Price

Cap Rate is an abbreviation for *capitalization rate*. Cap rate is measured in percent and is a measure of the income return of the property if you paid 100% cash (which no one does). The higher the cap rate for a property, the more yield per dollar invested; 8% cap is better than a 6% cap etc.

The second formula can be rewritten and inverted as a third related equation:

- Value of Property (\$) = NOI / Market Cap Rate

This is the formula that an appraiser uses to value a commercial income-producing property, it's called an income-based appraisal. Market Cap Rate is the prevailing average cap rate which the buying market accepts in a particular market. It's available from local brokers. Buying a property at the *market cap rate* means that you are paying the *retail price* for a property.

A "good deal" is when the cap rate at which you are buying the property is greater than the market cap rate. When you follow this, you are creating free equity. In a moment, I'll show you how much. As apartment entrepreneurs, *we provide value and earn money by both finding and offering properties in which the purchase cap rate is greater than the market cap rate.*

Notice that cap rate and value, are inversely related, meaning that as the cap rate goes up, the price or value goes down. It usually takes a little time for newbies to get their brain wrapped around this inverse relationship. But we are looking to buy at a cap rate higher than the market cap. The higher the cap, the lower the price.

Example: Analyzing Apartments

Here's an example: You find a 10-unit apartment which has rents of $500 per month and 90% occupancy. The expenses are $27,000 per year. The market cap rate is 8.5%. You can buy it for $270,000 and there is no rehab needed. Is that a good deal?

Remember, we want to buy at a cap rate higher than the market cap. That provides us free equity in the deal. It's a quick calculation that you can do on the back of an envelope:

Step #1: Determine the NOI:

• NOI ($/yr) = Revenue – Expenses

Revenue = 10 units x $500/mo x 12 months x 90%
Revenue = $54,000 / yr
Expenses = $27,000 / yr
NOI = $54,000 - $27,000 = **$27,000 / yr**

Remember to include the occupancy factor (90%) because an empty unit is a non-revenue unit. The property nets $27,000 per year after paying **ALL** expenses including the management fee, taxes, insurance, repairs and maintenance, etc. But remember, expenses do not include the mortgage payments. That comes later and I'll show you *Cash Flow* in just a moment.

Step #2: Determine the cap rate at this purchase price.

- Cap Rate (%) = NOI / Price

    NOI = $27,000 / yr
    Price = $270,000
    Cap Rate = $27,000 / $270,000 = **10%**

The purchase cap rate is 10%. It's what we call a "10 cap" deal. That means that if you were to pay all cash for this property (which no one does), you'd receive a 10% annual return on your cash, in the form of passive income. In a moment, I'll show you how to boost your return on cash in the deal, thru leverage.

Step #3: Is this a good deal?

The criterion for a good deal is that you purchase at a cap rate greater than the market cap.

- Good Deal: Purchase Cap Rate > Market Cap Rate

    Purchase Cap Rate = 10%
    Market Cap Rate = 8.5%
    10% > 8.5% so **Yes, this is a good deal**.

Because you can buy it a cap rate above the market cap rate, you are buying it at a price *below* the market value. Remember the inverse relationship between cap rate and price. You should buy this property or flip it.

How good of a deal is it? Well, let's quickly determine the market value:

- Value ($) = NOI / Market Cap Rate

  NOI = $27,000 / yr
  Market Cap Rate = 8.5%
  Value = $27,000 / 8.5% = **$317,000** (rounded off)

So, it's appraised value would be $317,000. You can buy it for $270,000 so you have $47,000 of free equity in the deal:

  Free Equity = $317,000 - $270,000 = **$47,000**

The greater the difference between the relative purchase cap rate and market cap rate, the greater the equity in the deal for you.

If you wanted to wholesale it, you'd market it at a price less than $317,000 so it would sell fast. You have to leave a "good deal" for your End-Buyer. If you sell it for $280,000, you'd net $10,000 on this single transaction.

  Wholesale Profit = $280,000 - $270,000 = **$10,000**

What if you wanted to buy it as an 11 cap deal, what's your maximum offer price?

- Price = NOI / Cap Rate

  NOI = $27,000 / yr
  Cap Rate = 11%
  Price = $27,000 / 11% = **$245,000** (rounded off)
  Free Equity = $317,000 - $245,000 = **$72,000**

Let's say you buy it at $270,000 to hold it. How much cash flow do you receive?

Cash Flow

I've pointed out that expenses do NOT include the mortgage payments, otherwise known as the *debt service payments*. The debt service payments are paid out of the NOI so cash flow is the difference between the NOI and the debt service payments. Here are the three final formulas:

- Cash Flow ($/yr) = NOI – Debt Service Payments
- Cash in the Deal = Down Payment + Closing Costs + Rehab Costs
- Cash-on-Cash Return (%) = Cash Flow / Cash in the Deal

Cash in the Deal includes the down payment, closing costs and any rehab capital needed to address the deferred maintenance. (If you are planning to add rehab capital to raise the occupancy or rents, then you need to re-evaluate the increased NOI at the higher rents and occupancy).

Cash-on-Cash Return is where it gets really exciting and points out the power of leverage in real estate. When you use financing (leverage) to buy a property, the *cash-on-cash return is always greater than the cap rate.*

Example: Cash Flow and Cash-on-Cash Return

Let's finish analyzing this 10-unit deal where you can purchase it for $270,000. If you buy it for 25% down with a mortgage at 5% interest and 25 year amortization, what is your *cash flow* and *cash-on-cash return*?

Step #4: Determine the Cash Flow:

- Cash Flow ($/yr) = NOI – Debt Service Payments

    NOI = $27,000 / yr

Loan Amount = 75% x $270,000 = $202,500
Debt Service = $1,184/mo x 12 = $14,208 / yr
Cash Flow = $27,000 - $14,208 = **$12,792/yr**

Step #5: Determine the Cash in the Deal and the Cash-on-Cash Return:

- Cash in the Deal ($) = Down Payment + Closing Costs + Rehab Costs
- Cash-on-Cash Return (%) = Cash Flow / Cash in the Deal

Down payment = 25% x $270,000 = $67,500
Closing Costs = $8,000
Rehab Costs = $0
Cash in the Deal = $67,500 + $8,000 + $0 = $75,500
Cash-on-Cash Return = $12,792 / $75,500 = **16.9%**

It's a 10 cap deal but the Cash-on-Cash return is 16.9%! That's the power of leverage in commercial income producing properties. You see that even if you buy it conventionally, you get *double digit* cash-on-cash returns passively. That's why apartments were created – to be income-producing properties.

There's one more important point on cash-on-cash return. As you reduce your Cash in the Deal, your Cash-on-Cash Return grows exponentially. When your Cash in the Deal is $0 and you have Cash Flow, your Cash-on-Cash Return is *infinite*.

Now, you may say, "I don't have the $75,000 or the credit for a new loan." Ok, does that stop you? No, I'm just showing the tremendous results for a *conventional purchase*. You could negotiate owner financing to reduce the down payment. You could raise the down payment from a self-directed IRA holder. You could raise a credit partner. These are just some of the techniques which I will teach you in Chapter 7.

Remember, you are the *entrepreneur* not the investor. Your job is to get things done using *other* people's resources.

If the Cash-on-Cash Return is 16.9%, then as long as you pay less than 16.9% interest for your private money, you have cash flow left over for yourself and you own the property nothing down. And your Cash-on-Cash return is *infinite*. Any improvements you make to boost NOI, go 100% to you. I did this on my very first small apartment.

That's just your return from income. Now, I'm about to show you the tremendous power of *forced appreciation* in creating equity, or your *net worth*.

But first, I want to give you a *"cheat sheet"* of all the formulas and the methodology I am teaching here you so you can use it on your own deals. Download it here.

Bonus Resource
Tool: *Apartment Deal Analysis Cheat Sheet*
www.BMSABook.com/sheet

Forced Appreciation Will Make You Wealthy

You now know how to analyze commercial apartments from an income basis. And I've shown that buying at a cap rate which is greater than the market cap rate creates free equity for you. Let me show you how the same formulas are used to create additional equity for you by modest operational improvements to your apartments. It's called *forced appreciation*.

DEFINITION: *Forced Appreciation is the process and attribute of increasing a commercial apartment property's value by raising the NOI.*

Remember, the formula I just taught you:

• Value = NOI / Market Cap Rate.

This is the same formula that professional appraisers use to evaluate and appraise commercial apartments. It's called an *income-based appraisal*. It's all about the NOI. ANYTHING which raises the NOI automatically boosts the value of a property. How do you raise the NOI? The simplest and fastest methods are raising the rent and/or raising the average occupancy. Each contributes to raising the NOI.

Given that, let's examine the process and leverage of *"capping out a property"* by forced appreciation. First by rent increases and then by occupancy increases.

EXAMPLE: Forced Appreciation by $10 Rent Increase

Let's say I raise the rents a very modest $10 per month on a property where the market cap is 8.5%. What does that do to the NOI and the increased "equity per door"? I'm going to *reword* the Value formula just slightly:

- Increased Value Per Door = Increased NOI / Market Cap Rate

  Increased NOI = $10/mo x 12 = $120 / yr *per door*
  Market Cap Rate = 8.5%
  Increased Value / Door = $120/8.5% = $1,411 / door

Now, for purposes of illustration, let's be conservative and assume just 85% average occupancy for the property:

Average Value Increase Per Door =
$1,411 x 85% = **$1,200 / door**

Which means that if I raise the rents just $10 per month across a property, I raise the value of the *entire complex by $1,200 per door!* Now, let's see how it's fun and what that means to you as you move to larger properties with more units.

Raise the Rent $10:

10 units x $1,200 / door = $12,000 new equity
50 units x $1,200 / door = $60,000
100 units x $1,200 / door = $120,000

That's all from just a $10 rent increase per door! Nobody decides to move out because of a $10 rent increase.

Make a $20 increase and you double these results. It's just simple math. You can predictably raise the value of your property thru operational improvements. But that's not the only way you can create forced appreciation. Raising the average occupancy is another way to boost the equity in your apartments.

EXAMPLE: Forced Appreciation by 2% Occupancy Increase

In this example, let's assume $500 average rent and a 2% occupancy increase. If just 2% more of the property pays you $500 per month, how does that translate into the Average Value Increase Per Door?

Increased NOI = $500 / month x 2% = $10 / month

Raising the occupancy is just like raising the rent. And I've already shown the math on how a $10 rent increase translates into increased equity of $1,200 per door. *So, for every 2% occupancy increase, you increase your property's equity $1,200 per door.*

Raise the Occupancy 2%:

10 units x $1,200 / door = $12,000 new equity
50 units x $1,200 / door = $60,000
100 units x $1,200 / door = $120,000

Increase the occupancy by 4% and you double these results. Of course, this can be in addition to your rent increases. If you simultaneously raise the rents $10 while raising the occupancy 2%, you increase your equity by $2,400 per door ($1,200 + $1,200)!

Raise the Rent $10 AND Raise Occupancy 2%:

10 units x $2,400 / door = $24,000 new equity
50 units x $2,400 / door = $120,000
100 units x $2,400 / door = $240,000

That's what's known as *"capping out a property."* This shows how you can affect five and six-figure equity improvements with just small operational improvements to your property (and which most apartments need). You do it with better asset management and/or slight curb appeal improvements (called putting *"lipstick on a pig"*).

For you rehabbers, start playing with the numbers where you buy really distressed and underperforming apartments and you can easily raise the rents $40 or raise the occupancy 10%, *or more*, and you see how you can affect seven-figure equity gains.

What this analysis also shows is that you will naturally want to transition into larger properties so that you can leverage the increased amount of doors in forced appreciation for those extra zeroes. It's all about *playing bigger*. But remember, I recommend you start with small apartments to get that critical first deal done.

Case Study - $255,000 Equity Gain with Forced Appreciation

Anil Sikri and Dale Steinman are two partners who purchased a 30 unit apartment in Columbus, Ohio. They met thru my mentoring program. This was their first apartment deal – their first *"olive out of the jar."* Dale lives in Kansas and Anil lives in Illinois – far away from the property. Their only prior real estate experience was that Dale owned rental houses.

They found the property on MLS; it was distressed due to poor management (it was self-managed by the owner for 25 years) and had some deferred maintenance. As a result, the tenants were largely not paying even though the rental amounts were below market rent. The obvious *value plays* were to add new management, improve the *curb appeal* thru modest capital improvements, raise the rents and change the tenant mix. It was a *turnaround* play – mostly one *of better management* and attention.

Seeing the opportunity, Dale and Anil placed the property under contract and purchased it for only $250,000, or approximately $8,300 per door. They estimated that it needed rehab amounting to $2,000 per door. So, after carrying costs, their total investment would be approximately $11,000 per door. Their exit strategy was to stabilize the property, raise the NOI and sell it at its new higher valuation, thru *forced appreciation*. They expect to be able to sell the stabilized property for $20,000 per door so their conservative profit expectation is $255,000.

When they took it to the banks for financing, the project was denied because the banks believed it was *"too good to be true."* So Dale and Anil funded it with their own leveraged funds, using home equity loans and loans against their retirement accounts.

They are pursuing the power of forced appreciation. You can hear their full interview with all the details at the Bonus Resource.

Bonus Resource
Interview: *$255,000 Equity Gain with Forced Appreciation*
www.BMSABook.com/forced

Leveraging Your Increased Equity

You've seen how you can create the equity in a predictable manner. You could sit on that equity but I personally don't like "dead equity." Dead equity is equity that is not working for you. So how can you cash-out and use this equity?

One thing you can do, of course, is sell the property at a higher price. Take your cash but you'd have a capital gains tax liability (which is not the worst thing). If you want to avoid the taxes, you'd do a 1031 Exchange (explained in Chapter 2) and use the cash as the down payment on a larger apartment; and repeat this process, but with extra zeroes.

Or you could refinance your property at its new higher value and pull out *cash tax-free*: a loan is not a taxable event. Now, realize that placing a new loan at a higher loan balance would raise your debt service payments and lower your cash flow on the property being refinanced, but you'd more than make up for it if you use the cash to buy another larger property and get more *combined* cash flow from *two* apartment buildings.

In Chapter 8, I'll show you the strategy of Leverage and Velocity. It's a strategy where you pull out your equity every two years to double and quadruple your holdings and grow your equity 1,300% over a short time period.

Remember, the income-based valuation approach and forced appreciation only exist in commercial properties, not residential ones. This predictable approach to valuation and wealth creation is yet another reason I started with apartments.

Gathering the Numbers

Congratulations! You now know the math portion of this business. It's that simple. You passed. And as you've seen, both the current and future valuation is based on the numbers. Working with commercial apartments is a formulaic science of analyzing the numbers, i.e. the financials. So where do the financials come from?

The numbers come primarily from two documents:

1. Profit and Loss Statement (P&L)
2. Rent Roll

The *Profit and Loss Statement* is a 12 month report that shows the trailing 12 month history of revenue, expenses, and NOI, broken down into monthly and cumulative results for the past 12 months. It's also called a *Trailing 12 Month P&L*, or *Income and Expense Statement*.

Looking at the financials on a historical monthly basis allows you to not only see the cumulative 12 month results but to also see variations in performance. You can quickly assess whether the property's performance is trailing up, down or neutral.

The *Rent Roll* is a current snapshot of how many units are occupied, who lives in each unit, the rent they pay, their move-in date, their lease expiration date and how much back rent they may owe. It allows you to not only determine the occupancy but also such things as the ebb and flow timing of new residents by their move-in dates, the paying quality of each resident by whether they are carrying a balance due, and if some residents are paying less than market rents.

Just like a business analyst can read any business thru its P&L, you can read an apartment business thru its Trailing 12 Months P&L and its Rent Roll. You use these documents to evaluate deals and make your offers on properties sight unseen. You also use these documents to assess the *"value plays"* – those opportunities to raise rents, boost occupancy or reduce expenses – perhaps thru a protest of the property tax valuation.

I need to make a final point about property valuations. You value properties and make offers based on *Actuals*, not *Pro-Forma* numbers. Actuals reflect the current state, the real numbers. Pro-forma are projected numbers and don't reflect the reality of today. Chase pro-forma numbers and you'll overpay.

This formulaic approach of receiving and reading P&L's and Rent Rolls on any property from *anywhere* is yet another reason why I chose apartments. This inherent numbers-based approach contributes to a business that you can do part-time.

You can analyze financials and make offers on your schedule, maybe at nights after work. You can assess turnaround situations based on the numbers and reliably *predict* your future profit. You don't need to see the property to evaluate it or make an offer.

Critical Success Factors

Success in real estate is about consistent, small, daily steps repeated over and over. Here are your critical success factors:

- Marketing for deals
- Marketing for dollars
- Making offers

People often ask, *"How long will it take me to do a deal?"* It's a very reasonable and logical question but really it's not one I can answer because I can't control your actions. But one thing I can say with certainty is that if you make no offers, you will make no money. That's why the mindset is so important and why I dedicate time to it in Chapters 9 and 10.

You also need to be able to recognize a *solid* apartment deal. Marketing is your business, but solid deals are your product. This is how you build your reputation and your credibility when you have no experience. Too many people try to enter this business unprepared and don't even understand the fundamentals you now know. Unknowingly, these unprepared newbies try to flip bad deals or ask investors to lend on bad deals. You may do this once but not a second time with the same buyer or investor. And wealth comes from being able to go back and repeat business with your existing relationships. That's why this chapter is important in showing you the valuation fundamentals of apartment properties for good deals.

Now you are ready to start finding deals to evaluate.

Coming Up...

In the next chapter, you are going to learn how to find the best deals, including off-market deals that are not even listed for sale yet.

Chapter Summary

- To begin, you simply need a phone, Internet access, a basic calculator, and sixth-grade math skills. You do not need an automobile.
- You have to know how to recognize a solid apartment deal, whether buying or wholesaling.
- Commercial apartments (5+ units) are evaluated based on the "numbers" – which makes them perfect for starting part-time and doing deals sight unseen in any city, even outside your own back yard.
- As a commercial broker once said, '"*Apartments are "real estate". Houses are "feel estate."'*
- To evaluate a deal, there are only three terms you need to understand: NOI, Cap Rate and Cash-on-Cash Return.

- A good deal is when the *Purchase Cap Rate* is greater than the *Market Cap Rate*. Buying at a Cap Rate greater than the Market Cap Rate creates free equity.
- Cash-on-Cash return is significantly multiplied when you buy a property with 3rd party financing.
- You buy on Actuals NOT Pro-Forma – using two documents: 1) Trailing 12 Months P&L and 2) Rent Roll; making offers sight unseen.
- Forced Appreciation is the ability to predictably boost a property's value by operational improvements.
- Every $10 rent increase translates into equity gains of $1,200 per door. Every 2% occupancy increase translates into equity gains of another $1,200 per door.
- Forced Appreciation is how you can create predictable five-figure, six-figure and even seven-figure wealth increases, which you can leverage into cash or buying more apartments, tax free.
- Your three critical success factors are:
    1. Marketing for deals
    2. Marketing for dollars
    3. Making offers

Bonus Resources Summary

Tool: *Apartment Deal Analysis Cheat Sheet*
www.BMSABook.com/sheet

Interview: *$255,000 Equity Gain with Forced Appreciation*
www.BMSABook.com/forced

Chapter 6

How to Find the Deals

In the last chapter, you learned how to evaluate good commercial apartment deals, based on the numbers, and anywhere across the country (or world) sight unseen.

And as I've emphasized throughout the book, you are not in the real estate business. You are in the *marketing business* and you are always marketing for two things: *deals and dollars.* So this chapter is about marketing for the deals.

An important point is that your business begins with deal flow, not dollars. I repeat, *it begins with deal flow.* The type of deal will dictate the primary strategy for the property: wholesale, buy and hold or rehab. Don't make the mistake that I've observed with some newbies who proclaim, *"If I just had some buyers, I'd be all set."* Wrong. Your real value is established in finding the deals.

Given that, how do you start creating your deal flow? Well, there are a myriad of ways but here are the three primary methods I use:

- **Method #1**: Real Estate Listing Services
- **Method #2**: Commercial Brokers and Agents
- **Method #3**: Direct Mail

Bonus Resource
Webinar: *How to Make Big Money in Small Apartments*
www.BMSABook.com/bmsa

Method #1: Real Estate Listing Services

There are numerous websites which provide listings of apartments for sale. Just as with any listing service, they list apartments which are *on the market* for sale. The listing will always have the basic information such as the address, asking price, and contact information – whether a broker or sale by owner. Most of the time, it's listed by a broker.

In the commercial real estate world, a big listing service is a website called Loopnet.com, it is essentially an MLS (multiple listing service) for commercial listings of all types and sizes, including multifamily properties. It is free and it covers North America.

For example, you can go to Loopnet.com, type in any city or zip code of interest, check the box for "Multifamily" and listings of apartments on the market for sale are presented.

No matter the listing service, each listing will vary on the amount of detailed financials provided on the website. If they are not available, you call the contact on the listing and ask for them. Remember to ask for the "Actuals."

I've done deals which I found from listing services and I've had students who've done deals from listing services, including some of the Case Studies documented in this book. But, let me tell you right now that if you're using listing services as your exclusive, or even primary, source of deal flow, you're going to become frustrated and probably quit (which I don't want for you).

You see, the listing services mostly include the "retail-priced deals," not the good deals. The properties listed are generally being sold at the market cap rate. Of course, you can negotiate the price down or negotiate for flexible financing but don't rely on listing services as your primary source of deal flow.

In practice, listing services are best for checking a market, practicing your newly acquired deal analysis skills and finding brokers.

Method #2: Commercial Brokers and Agents

A better source for deal flow is commercial brokers. Obviously, commercial brokers have listings of apartments for sale. But I want you to realize that you can also get access to *small apartments* from *realtors* – the distinction being that realtors primarily deal in houses but some will also list small apartments, even up to 50+ units. In this chapter, I am going to use the term, "broker" as a catch-all term to mean commercial agents or residential realtors.

Now when brokers have a good deal come across their desk, do you think the first thing they do is broadly post their newly found good deal on a listing service? No, they don't. So what do they do with it?

They first contact their "people" - their *private* buyer's list of apartment players who they already know and have a *relationship* with; the people who have *demonstrated* they know the business. Brokers save their good deals for them and present to them first. (Don't worry. In a moment, I'm going to show you how to get on their preferred list).

Here's an example of the type of calls you'll receive when you have a great broker relationship, "*Lance, this is Adam over at Houston Commercial Realty. I just came out of our Thursday staff meeting and there's a new apartment deal that came in. You've got to jump on this. I'm emailing you over the information packet now.*" This is taken from an actual call I received from a broker, someone who I had never purchased from but had established a relationship.

These good deals are called "*pocket listings*" – going back to the old days when brokers carried the paper listings around in their jacket pocket. Brokers generally place the property on a listing service only after they've exhausted their private contact list with the pocket listing.

Why do brokers horde good deals? Because of the simple economics that they only get paid commissions on deals that close and they want to selectively present their pocket listings to people who have shown they understand the apartment industry and can presumably close – so the broker gets paid. And frankly, they don't want to waste time with *untrained* newbies.

So, if brokers save the "pocket listings" for the people who they have a *relationship* with, what do you want to have with brokers? That's right, a relationship. And now I'm going to show you how to develop a relationship with a broker *quickly*, even when you're new and have *no prior experience*. It's all done over the phone and anyone can do it. I have an 18 year old student who can even do this.

First, I'll explain how to find the brokers who have the type of pocket deals you are targeting. Then, I'll show you how to call them and get on their private buyer's list so they are sending deals to you.

Finding Brokers with Apartment Deals

Let's say you are looking for a good small apartment deal in Memphis, Tennessee. You want to find local brokers who have pocket listings of small apartments. Here's what you do.

You go to any on-line listing service; I'll assume Loopnet for this case but there are many. Type in the city of interest to you; in this example, Memphis, Tennessee. You then select the box for multifamily, click "Search" and you receive a listing of apartments for sale in Memphis, Tennessee.

You sort through the listings based upon your particular buying criteria (small, medium, large, cap rate, days on market, fixer-uppers, etc.) to narrow the group to your specific parameters. Remember though, we are not looking for listings in this process. We are looking for brokers. You don't have to be exact.

If you are looking for *small apartments*, this process will produce a list of small apartments on the market in Memphis. The brokers who list those properties are local brokers which market small apartments similar to what you want. If they have small apartments on the listing service, *there's a good chance they have small apartment pocket listings that have not been listed.* Those are the ones we are going after – the pocket listings.

Note the name and phone number of the agents who are listing these properties. And go ahead and print their listing with the property information. You'll need it in the next step.

That's the process of finding a broker. You can find brokers anywhere in the country doing this. The next step is how to call the broker.

Secret to Successful Broker Calls

It's time for the call. Your objective with your first broker call is to develop a relationship with them so they will send you their pocket listings. You know the old saying, *"You only get one chance to develop a first impression."* It's true here. On your first call, you position your credibility. Act like a pro and you're labeled a pro. Act like an amateur and you're labeled an amateur.

If you're like me when I first started, I was terrified of the prospect of getting on the phone and speaking with brokers (or sellers). After all, I assumed they were light years ahead of me since I was just a trained newbie. What I have since discovered (and you will too) is that they are just like you and me. They have their own daily challenges like everyone else and they just want to sell real estate so they can provide for their families. And this is important... they *need* your business.

That's why a call from someone who doesn't sound like an absolute uneducated amateur is a breath of fresh air to a broker. They see you as another potential client. Most of the calls they receive are from untrained wanna-be's, so the bar is actually set low for you in achieving a successful broker call.

Here's how you do it – and this works perfectly, even if you have absolutely *no experience* in real estate of any kind. I've had hundreds of students report back how this process worked for them on their *very first* broker call.

There are two essential secrets to your broker calls:

- **Secret #1:** Ask high quality questions
- **Secret #2:** Use precise language

Secret #1: Ask High Quality Questions

Keep in mind, you are on the phone. All the broker has to gauge you is the tone of your voice and the quality of your questions. I know you are probably concerned that the broker is going to ask you questions like: *"What is your experience?", "How much down payment do you have?", "Do you have a Proof of Funds?"* That's natural, but stop. It's just your Little Voice talking.

So, how do you prevent a broker from asking you these questions you want to avoid? Answer: <u>You ask the questions</u>. But you have to ask good ones. Not only do you *control the conversation* but through the quality of your questions you *position* yourself as someone who knows the business. Demonstrate knowledge and they will assume you've been in the business for years. And that's all you have to do.

I'm sure you're probably thinking, *"What questions should I ask?"*

Recall in the previous step of finding brokers that I instructed you to print the listings you found in your search for brokers. You are going to ask insightful questions about their listing. You are going to ask about the cap rate, the occupancy, the market rents, the value plays - all the things I taught you in Chapter 5 on how to size up a good deal. The deeper the questions, the deeper you ingrain in their mind that you know what you are doing. It's all about positioning yourself. What you don't want to do is ask about the decor of the kitchens – that's a house type of question.

The quality of the questions you ask *signal* to others whether you know your business or not. And when you pass this hurdle, you will discover the brokers open up quite easily. But once you're positioned, how do you now get the pocket listings? That leads to the second secret for a successful call.

Secret #2: Use Precise Language

During your questioning, you may assess that the public listing you called about is actually a good candidate deal, worthy of investigation. If that's the case, you ask for the financials and you run the numbers like I showed you in Chapter 5, and you make an offer.

Now, the odds are that the public listing is not really a good deal. Remember, we don't expect to find too many good deals on the listing services. Those are the left-over deals. You are going for the pocket listings and you want to get yourself on the broker's private buyer's list so he's sending you the good stuff. Here's how you do it.

The human brain craves *specificity*. So Secret #2 of your call is to precisely describe the types of deals you are seeking. The more precisely you speak to a broker, not only do you further position yourself but you also create in their mind a vivid image of the type of properties you are looking to purchase. They also assume you have been doing the business for years because they only hear this precise language from the pros.

Even if the deal you initially called about is the deal of a lifetime, you make sure to describe the type of deals you are looking for - in precise language. When I do this live at my seminars and in front of an audience, on open microphone, it never ceases to amaze me how a call on a so-so deal will completely transform when I start explaining what I'm really looking for.

The broker's brain hears the specificity it seeks and they naturally start telling me about their *other* deals. They'll say, "*You know, two other deals come to mind that you probably want to look at. Give me your email and I'll send you the financials.*" Keep in mind that, at my seminars, these are blind calls to Loopnet listings provided by the audience. The brokers don't know me. Precise language and clarity in communication with brokers is power. The brokers completely open up – on the very first call. Many times at my seminars I find that I have to cut the call short just for the sake of time at the event.

Broker Scripts

You need to use a script with every broker call – especially on the initial contact. This is not an area where you just "wing it" because you believe you are good talker. Scripts provide you confidence while establishing a rhythm where you control the conversation. And the ability to rattle off a list of sequential and intelligent questions signals to the broker that you know your business.

This leads to the next point, *what type of precise language do you use?* In a moment, I'll share an extract from my actual script. If we ever work together, I'll give you the complete time-tested script that I and thousands of students have validated. You literally just follow it. If you're developing your own, just use the recipe I am revealing here. An untested script under development is better than no script.

By the way, when I do broker calls in front of live audiences, I make a point of following my script <u>verbatim</u> – just to prove the power of the language. If the broker happens to ask me a question that's not on the script, I act like I didn't hear him and go back to my scripted questions and precise language. The audience always laughs when they see how the conversation comes back under my control. Again, it's the power of clarity in your language. So let's come back to what to say…

Here's an extract from my script which you can use:

Trained Newbie: *"Let me tell you the type of deals I'm looking for. I'm looking for small apartments of 2-30 units. Something that has a value play associated with it: maybe it needs repositioning, or new management, maybe a change in the tenant mix or just an increase in the rents or occupancies. Rehabs are okay. Vacant properties are also okay but no war zone areas. Do you have something like that?"*

Now, in contrast, here's the language of an untrained newbie:

Untrained Newbie: *"Do you have any good deals?"*

Admittedly, with the latter, I'm probably oversimplifying for contrast and laughs but I want to make the point that the bar has been set low for you. You can easily get over it and be successful – when you use these secrets. And when brokers receive a call like this, they size up the caller as an untrained newbie and immediately go into their *qualifying* questions: *"What is your experience?"*, *"How much down payment do you have?"*, *"Do you have a Proof of Funds?"*

You Don't Need Proof of Funds

Those qualifying questions are automatic because the caller betrayed the fact that they really don't know the business. The broker is just trying to politely get them off the phone. Brokers are not here to train, they are here to close deals.

On the topic of Proof of Funds, let me tell you this. Only once have I ever used a Proof of Funds. And that's because I had a 7-figure Proof of Funds from a buyer and I decided it would be fun to use it. Other than that single occurrence, I have <u>never</u> been asked for a Proof of Funds. Proof of Funds is a qualifying vehicle for people who the broker suspects don't know what they are doing. You are going to qualify yourself by 1) the quality of your questions and 2) your use of precise language. Do this and they don't ask. They don't need to.

Follow this process using my script, or one you develop, and you'll have a string of successful first broker calls. And then once you've had a successful initial call, you make sure and stay in contact with the broker so you stay on his or her radar screen for future deals.

Let's see how an 18 year old and his dad made $30,000 following this process.

Case Study – 18 Year Old Makes $30,000

Dan and Dylan Badinghaus are a father and son real estate team. Dylan is 18 years old. Together, they had done some house rehabs on the side and owned some rental houses but they decided to play bigger with small apartments. As part of the partnership, 18 year old Dylan held the role of calling brokers and developing the relationships for receiving pocket listings. Dylan was trained so he called brokers using a script with high quality questions and precise language. Dan practiced with Dylan three times and set Dylan out to work the phone.

Out of those broker relationships, they closed their first apartment deal. They live in Indiana but their very first apartment deal was a 36-unit flip in Ohio. The property was an off-market bank foreclosure that had fallen out of closing because the buyer couldn't close. How did they know this? Because on one of their follow-up calls to their brokers, they heard these magic words, *"I'm glad you called, I just learned of a deal this afternoon that fell out of closing. It's a great deal and you need to jump on this right now."*

Overnight, they analyzed the deal and made an offer the next morning. It was a pretty simple analysis because the asking price was so low. They placed the property under contract with a very short timeline imposed by the bank. They canvassed their contacts and within two days, they found a buyer – a first-time apartment buyer - who had the cash to close. Their buyer put up the earnest money, quickly conducted the due diligence with Dan and Dylan's help so that the deal closed in *nine business days* (the current record amongst my students). The profit was $30,000.

There's lots of cool things about this deal and the achievement of Dan and Dylan. Of course, the $30,000 is pretty cool. Closing in nine business days is amazing but what impresses me the most is the fact that an 18 year old followed the process and developed the broker relationships leading to a $30,000 flip fee on his very first deal.

Can you imagine your life today if you had known what I'm teaching when you were just 18? I can only imagine; I didn't get started until I was nearly 40. It's a testament to Dan for getting this type of financial-empowering education for his young son.

Read what Dylan wrote:

"The scripts are awesome. I'm 18 years old and I can talk to brokers like I've been doing it for years. I even show them up some times. If a kid like me can do it, anybody should be able to."
-- Dylan Badinghaus

I always tell this story because I know my biggest fear in getting started was talking to brokers and sellers. And it's a big fear for others – perhaps you. If an 18 year old kid can call brokers successfully, so can you.

Method #3: Direct Mail

This all leads to the third way you're going to generate apartment deal flow, and the most powerful. It is direct mail. Direct mail is the most under-utilized secret weapon there is when it comes to marketing for deals. One of the reasons it is so effective is because so few people do it. It takes some expense but not a lot. It takes effort but you can outsource and automate it all thru systems.

Direct mail essentially is where you mail a letter or post card to apartment owners. The direct mail piece conveys the basic message, "If you're interested in selling, I'm interested in buying." And those owners that have some level of motivation to sell will call or email you.

And with so much advertising on-line these days, direct mail usage has dropped so that direct mail response rates have increased. Keep in mind it's all a numbers game. We have some campaigns that deliver 3-5% call response consistently (the national average is 1%). We have others that deliver over a 20% call response!

There is no cold calling. It is all *in-bound calls*. You speak only to people who are responding to you, i.e. they are pre-qualified leads. They pre-qualify themselves by the simple fact that they took time to contact you. The direct mail piece does all of the sales work. They are like *little sales soldiers* out there 24/7 looking for motivated sellers for you.

Let's look in detail at how direct mail benefits you:

- **Benefit #1**: Access to off-market and pre-foreclosure deals
- **Benefit #2**: No competition
- **Benefit #3**: One-on-one access to the seller
- **Benefit #4**: Creative deals

Benefit #1: Access to Off-Market and Pre-Foreclosure Deals

Off-market deals are deals where the property is not listed for sale. About 95% of the inbound calls I and my students receive are from owners who don't have the property listed for sale. They were *thinking about selling* and our little sales soldier intersected with their thinking so we get the call first. Even if the owner does not call right away, they will often file the direct mail piece in their property file and when their situations changes, they make the call.

Rather than combing the listing services like EVERYONE does to find deals, this is another way – besides pocket listings – to get access to deals that no one else knows about. As the fisherman, you don't want to fish where everyone else is fishing; you want to fish in your secret fishing hole. That's what direct mail provides – a figurative secret fishing hole for deal flow.

A specific type of off-market deal is a pre-foreclosure; they're great. Pre-foreclosures are small apartments that are behind on payments but have not yet progressed into a foreclosure process. Obviously, the owners are motivated to sell. Want to know how to get access to pre-foreclosure deals? Use direct mail and you'll get the lead before anyone else.

Benefit #2: No Competition

Because 95% of calls from direct mail respondents are not currently on the market, that means no competition from other buyers. The benefits of this for you are self-evident.

Benefit #3: One-on-One Access to the Seller

A really powerful result of direct mail is that it puts you in *direct* conversation with the owner. You can understand the reasons for their motivation so that you can structure win-win deals that satisfy their needs while leaving you with a good deal for purchase or flip. And with direct conversation, there is less chance of miscommunication or bias that might occur when speaking through a broker. After all, brokers are human and they see the world one way – which might not coincide with ours. Given a choice, you much prefer to present your offer directly to the owner. Let me give an example.

Example: Grapevine

Have you ever played or heard of the party game called Grapevine? In Grapevine, you line people up. At one end of the line, someone whispers a message to the person on the end. And then that person whispers the message to the person next to them; then that person does the same with their neighbor, until the message is relayed person-by-person down the line. When the person at the opposite end is asked to repeat the message, what happens?

The message is completely transformed from the original message. That's because of internal and subconscious interpretation filters which are applied by each person in the chain. There is an accumulation of error in the message that pops out at the end of the daisy chain.

This grapevine effect is inherent to human communication with multiple parties. That's why you prefer to speak directly. Now, if a sellers' agent is already involved, you have to work through them, recognizing and guarding against miscommunication. But let's say you introduce your own buyer's agent. Now there are four parties to the transaction: *you, your buyer's agent, the seller's agent,* and the *seller*. What happens? You created your own game of Grapevine with *your real estate deal*. So don't do that. Don't think you need a buyer's agent. You don't.

Most newbies who enlist a buyer's agent do it as a crutch to avoid the fear of having to directly speak to someone. They think, *"If I just speak to my buddy, Sam, the broker, he'll do all of my talking for me and I'll get a good deal."* Wrong. Until you get at least your first deal under your belt, you should not use a buyer's agent because there is very, very high probability the deal will fall apart due to the Grapevine effect. Now, once you start to develop your systems, then you can perhaps add a buyer's agent. By then, you have gone through the process at least once and you can train someone to follow your proven protocol.

So starting out, you prefer only two people in the conversation: you and the seller. You'll accept three if there's a seller's agent involved. Even then, you can ask to speak directly with the owner. Let's look at the final benefit of direct mail.

Benefit #4: Creative Deals

When you have a one-on-one conversation with an owner and you understand what their motivation is and what problem you need to solve, now you can craft a very creative deal. When one-on-one, you don't need to rely on a broker to present your creative offer to a seller. In fact, you prefer they don't. Think about it. When there's a go-between, you're counting on the seller's agent to sell your offer. You're counting on them to understand it. They may present it but they may not *sell* it.

The most creative deals are done when you can talk one-on-one with the owner. Let me give you an example of all of the above benefits using the Case Study of my very first deal.

Case Study – 100% Owner Financing from Direct Mail

As an absolute green, but trained newbie, I did my first marketing campaign to create deal flow using direct mail. I sent out 50 letters to out-of-state owners of small apartments in Houston, Texas – where I live. One of those out-of-state owners who responded was Ms. Mansson. She had owned her Houston four-plex for two years, held it free and clear (no mortgage) and she lived in Honolulu. It was her first and only real estate deal - which she bought at someone else's recommendation. She had no knowledge of apartments but she did have a management company. The property was not listed.

On my very first conversation with Ms. Mansson, I asked her, *"Ms. Mansson, why are you considering selling?"* She replied candidly, *"I bought this property two years ago because I wanted to receive a <u>monthly check</u>. And I don't want to have to speak with anyone. I don't want to have to review management reports; I don't want to have to approve capital improvements. I just want a monthly check. So I want to sell it."*

What did I hear that Ms. Mansson wanted? What problem did I need to solve? She just wanted a monthly check without ever speaking to anyone. If I could solve that problem, I'd have my first deal from my first direct mail campaign.

So I said, *"Ms. Mansson, what about if I sent you a monthly check and you never heard from me again in life? How would that be for you?"* Her response, *"What do you mean?"*

I explained, *"You sell me your property and I'll send you a monthly mortgage check. As the new owner, I'll deal with the management company. You'll never have to speak with anyone and you'll receive a monthly check."*

She said yes and that deal closed within 30 days. Now, what type of financing did I negotiate? That's right, seller financing; she took her purchase in installment payments. How much down payment did I give her? None. How much did she ask for? None. All she wanted was a monthly check.

That's the power of direct mail for you. Let me ask you this question. If Ms. Mansson had her property listed and an agent was involved, do you think I would have gotten the same deal? Very unlikely. The agent's first question would have been, *"Where's my commission in this offer?"* And he would have most likely *unsold* my offer. She accepted my first and only offer to her.

Remember, I was trained but totally new to the business. Ms. Mansson never asked me about my credit. She never asked for my financial statement. She never asked about my experience. How is that?

One reason is that motivated sellers are more interested in solving their problem. The second reason has to do with how I positioned myself on the call – just like I taught you with brokers. And I'll teach you in a moment for sellers.

I'm such an advocate for direct mail that I want to give you two more Case Studies to make the point, drawn from my own files.

Case Study - $13,100 from Direct Mail

Here's another deal of mine that came about from direct mail. An owner of a triplex called me one time and said he received my direct mail piece and was interested in selling. His reason was that he wanted to use the proceeds to buy a larger property. At the time, I wasn't interested in owning a triplex but I thought to myself, *"Maybe I can flip it."* (Remember my mantra: *Always Be Wholesaling*).

So I asked him, *"How much are you asking for your triplex?"* He thought about it and replied, *"$215,000."* I knew nothing about his property or its value so I gave him my automatic response, *"$215,000?! What makes you think it's worth that?"*

His answer got my attention. He explained, *"Well, my next door neighbor offered me $250,000 for it 6 months ago."* Bingo. My brain rushed to an obvious strategy for the property: I'd get it under contract and flip it to his neighbor. I ended up putting it under contract for $201,500. I ultimately flipped the contract to a local apartment renter who wanted to own her own place and I netted $13,100 on that direct mail campaign – all to the knowledge of my seller.

I need to share an educational point about how I found my buyer. Of course, the first person I contacted about buying my contract was the neighbor. Unfortunately, she had spent her spare cash on a land deal and thus was no longer in a position to buy the triplex. I eventually enlisted a realtor who found my buyer. (The realtor made $11,000 commission. I netted $13,100 after paying his commission).

But when I initially met the realtor at the property, I learned that *he had been the agent who originally sold my seller the property*. I could tell he was more than a little curious as to why he hadn't gotten a call from his client to list the property. I knew why. I got there first with my direct mail. And my little sales soldier intersected with that seller's internal conversation about selling his property.

Case Study – 50-Unit Bargain from Direct Mail

Here's a final direct mail example; also drawn from my files. I received a call from a letter campaign where this time the caller was looking to sell his 50 unit apartment. He had done a complete rehab over a couple of years – taking the property from boarded up to high occupancy. He had had a partner but he had bought him out. His reason for selling was that he co-owned the property with his wife – correction, his now ex-wife – and while the ink dried on their divorce papers, they wanted to remove all entanglements.

He explained that he had listed the property on Loopnet, admittedly at a high price just to see *"what would happen."* He had since taken it off of Loopnet. It was not currently listed anywhere and he never had an agent. On that first call, he told me his bottom-line price. I ran the numbers; the deal made sense at his price so I made him an immediate offer a little below his "bottom-line price" just so he'd have the satisfaction of negotiating me back up. I put it under contract and closed it in 60 days – with not another buyer in sight.

Why Do Owners Sell Real Estate at a Discount?

I showed you those three Case Studies to make the point of the benefits of direct mail and to address another question that pestered me when I started. And I get this question a lot so I want to answer it. The question is, *"Why do owners sell at a discount and why do they accept creative financing?"*

The answer is, *"It doesn't matter. They just do."* The more sophisticated answer is they do it for lots of reasons. I showed three different reasons just above in the Case Studies.

Back when I first started and before I got my mindset right, I'd spend all of my time trying to answer this question rather than doing my marketing. I had to somehow rationalize it. I guess I couldn't believe that someone would do it. The fact is they do.

This is a numbers game. We send out our letters and wait to see what comes back. Those that come back will tell us their reasons – not that the reasons are all that important. Just move forward with the knowledge and confidence that the deals are out there - waiting to hear from your little sales soldiers.

There's one last thing to cover, speaking with sellers.

Secret to Successful Seller Calls

You sent out your first direct mail. You may then be thinking, *"Uh-oh. Now what? What do I do when they call?"* I understand because that's the way I felt on my first campaign. Well, the answer parallels what I taught you about speaking with brokers so I am going to supplement that teaching with some unique points about speaking with sellers. If you skipped the section on "Secret to Successful Broker Calls" above, you should probably go back and read it.

First, just as with your first broker calls, your lack of experience or lack of financial depth has little to do with your success in negotiating deals with sellers. Recall my Case Study above on my first deal, a four-plex: 100% owner financing and the seller never asked about my credit, my experience or my financials. That's because I positioned myself well – even on my very first call with a seller.

As with your broker calls, you should be prepared for a seller call – use a Seller's Script. Keep it with you. Don't just "wing it" – especially when you are starting out. If you ever work with me, I'll give you mine. If you want to develop one on your own, here are two essential secrets to your seller calls:

- **Secret #1:** Ask about their property first
- **Secret #2:** Ask about their situation last

Follow this method and you'll develop rapport with your seller. They'll like you and trust you. The best deals that I've ever had and I've assisted my students with are the ones where there was a good relationship with the seller.

Secret #1: Ask About Their Property First

You don't want to start probing into someone's personal problems at the outset of the call. Instead, you ask a number of high quality questions about their property so that you position yourself as someone knowledgeable, while building rapport. Sellers tend to be less sophisticated than brokers so the bar is even lower here than with broker calls.

When I follow my Seller Script and call sellers live in front of an audience, I've actually had them reply, *"I'm not sure what that means."* One gentleman told me once, *"Those are good questions. I feel like I'm not giving you good answers."* (He also initially said he wouldn't accept seller financing but within 24 hours, he agreed to my offer of 100% seller financing - due to the rapport we developed over the first phone call).

So you just need to ask innocuous questions about the number of units, the rents, any deferred maintenance, etc. Start with the easy questions first; they feel more comfortable with you when you let them demonstrate they know the answers. Don't ask them on the first question, "What's the cap rate?" The answers are important but you are really using this questioning period to develop the relationship.

And when you are prepared, and follow a script, there is a rhythm to the questioning that positions you as very knowledgeable. They assume you've been in the business for years. And when you ask questions, you control the conversation. You'll find that they naturally begin to open up – especially if they are motivated. And the more they open up, the more of a relationship you're developing.

Secret #2: Ask About Their Situation Last

You've gotten thru the batch of questions about the property. Maybe you've even done some quick mental calculations about whether there is a deal here for you or not. And it looks like a good candidate for investigation. You've naturally developed rapport because you are asking the seller good questions about something that is interesting to them. (As a mentor taught me once, the secret to being interesting is to be *interested* in the other person).

Now is the time to find out their situation and probe a little bit. You want to know why they're selling and what they think they need so you can begin to structure a deal that addresses their problem. Want to know the secret to finding out why somebody is interested in selling? Here it is... *Ask*.

Newbies sometimes wonder if it's polite or proper to ask someone why they are selling. Not only is it proper but it's necessary. Just say, *"May I ask why you are considering selling?"* And they'll tell you. It's that simple. If they are really motivated, they will go into depth with the explanation – sometimes telling you more than you want to know about them.

From there, you can start considering the type of offer you can make to meet their needs while leaving a good deal for you.

Case Study – The Secret to 100% Owner Financing

Kenneth Hogans is a mortgage broker. He had never done a real estate deal previously but he set his goal to have an apartment deal done within a few months. So he launched a direct mail campaign using the letters I armed him with. With his first 50 letters, he received 18 calls. Out of those calls, he followed my Seller's Script and landed a nice five-unit apartment building in California with 100% owner financing.

When I asked Kenneth the secret to owner financing, he replied, *"Ask!"* Being in direct conversation with the owner facilitated that. It was his first deal and not only was it critical to him, it was also critical in demonstrating to his wife that the system worked. As Kenneth said, *"Direct mail beats any other advertising I've ever done in business."* You can hear the full interview at the Bonus Resource.

Bonus Resource
Interview: *The Secret to 100% Owner Financing*
www.BMSABook.com/ken

That's it. Remember, <u>your business begins with deal flow</u>. Follow the recipes I've just given you. Embedded in these recipes is over a decade of experience across my deals and hundreds of students' deals to help you quickly get your critical first deal done.

Coming Up…

In the next chapter, you'll learn the secret formula for funding any real estate transaction using none of your own cash or credit.

Chapter Summary

- You are in the marketing business. You market for *deals and dollars* – this chapter is about finding the deals.
- Your business begins with deal flow.

- Because deal analysis is based on the "numbers," your market is the United States (huge territory); you can start in your own backyard but you're not limited to it.
- Don't worry about why people sell property at a discount or why they accept creative financing; they just do. This is a numbers game.
- There are three primary sources of apartment deal flow:
  1. Listing services
  2. Brokers
  3. Direct mail
- Listing services are generally better for finding brokers than finding good deals.
- You want to develop relationships with brokers so you receive their "pocket listings."
- The secret to speaking with brokers is to:
  1. Ask high quality questions
  2. Use precise language
- You don't need a buyer's agent to start. It contributes to miscommunication and broken deals as a result of the Grapevine effect.
- Direct mail is the most under-utilized secret weapon in creating deal flow. The benefits are:
  1. Access to off-market deals
  2. No competition
  3. One-on-one access to the seller
  4. Creative deals
- The secret to speaking with sellers is to:
  1. Ask about their property first
  2. Ask about their situation last
- Be prepared. Use scripts for your broker calls and seller calls.

Bonus Resources Summary

Webinar: *How to Make Big Money in Small Apartments*
www.BMSABook.com/bmsa

Interview: *The Secret to 100% Owner Financing*
www.BMSABook.com/ken

Chapter 7

How to Fund the Deals

As another reminder, you are in the marketing business; you market for *deals and dollars*. In the previous chapter, I revealed the recipe for creating your deal flow. Now, it's time you learned about marketing for *dollars* – specifically private investors for your buy and hold apartments.

The biggest fear that keeps the vast majority of beginning real estate entrepreneurs from realizing their financial dreams is the fear over how to get the money for their deals. And the biggest fear that limits experienced real estate entrepreneurs is how to get larger funds for larger deals and/or expanding their business.

Whether you're looking to fund $6,000 or $6,000,000, you need to exercise the power of leverage in real estate by using other people's money (OPM). Here's a story that I think will impress you.

Case Study – Multimillionaire Wants to Use OPM

I received a call once from a gentleman who had been following my webinars on apartments and raising private money. He said, *"Lance, I really enjoy your webinars. I've recently sold my business and I'm looking to buy some apartments and, given your network of students, I thought you might be able to help me find a good one."* I thanked him and replied that I probably could. He then explained that he was looking for large apartment complexes, up to $10 million.

At that point, I politely asked the all-important qualifying question, *"Is this your money or do you have a pool of investors?"*

His replay caught my attention. He said, *"No, it's just me. My wife has given me an allotment of money to go out and buy apartments. I'm limited by a fixed amount so when I spend it, that's all I get. And I've been impressed with your webinars on how you can structure creative finance deals with OPM. I'm hoping that you can guide me in being able to do the same – to stretch my dollars. You see, my cash is limited to $15 million."*

My response, *"Excuse me?"* He repeated, *"Yea, I'm limited to $15 million and I'm looking to stretch my dollars and acquire as much property I can with my cash."*

That impressed me. Besides his $15 million allowance, it struck me that whether you have $1,500 or $15 million, everyone wants to stretch their dollars – to leverage them. It's part of the *7 Keys* I taught you in Chapter 2.

Case Study – Two Unemployed Partners Raise $6 Million, Revisited

In Chapter 2, I shared the Case Study of Denon Williams and Terry Warren, two real estate partners. I want to revisit them here as a prequel to what you're about to learn. In this chapter, I'll be referring back to them in more detailed Case Studies.

As review, when I first met them, they were both unemployed, as a result of a recent lay-off. They had no prior real estate experience, yet in their first 10 months, they purchased $6 million of real estate – using none of their own cash, none of their own credit and with no prior experience. It was a tremendous feat for absolute green – but trained – newbies.

How is that possible? They followed a formula, my Raising Private Money Formula.

This chapter reveals the secrets to raising all of the private money you will ever need for your real estate deals – small, medium or large. Profoundly simple, its brilliance is in its application for larger deals – paving the way for financial freedom in the shortest possible time.

Bonus Resource
Webinar: *How to Raise Huge Money in Today's Economy*
www.BMSABook.com/rpm

So how do you raise private money?

Raising Private Money Formula

Well, it's through the use of a four-part formula. And this actually came to me as a result of learning how to raise private money to buy a business. These four parts are remarkably straight-forward. And yet most people don't know there are four parts, let alone what the four parts are. If you miss any one of the four, you hinder your chances of raising private money.

On the other hand, if you master and apply all four – and make this your business to know and do – you will have access to all of the private money you'll ever need to do more real estate deals or to acquire or expand a business that does deals for you.

The purpose of this chapter is to expose you to the powerful four-part formula. Its application is truly unlimited. And rather than giving you a single fish, my contribution to your real estate success is to teach you how to fish. This tutorial is your lesson on fishing for money - what bait to use and how to make your offers extremely attractive (to the right kinds of fish).

So, prepare to have your real estate horizons broadened as you learn the four-part formula for raising private money, and its applications.

Here are the four parts to the Raising Private Money Formula:

- **Part 1**: Predisposed
- **Part 2**: Control
- **Part 3**: Low Risk
- **Part 4**: High Return

Before I explain each part, let me emphasize that *you have to use all four parts <u>simultaneously</u>. The power of the formula is that it speaks to the psychology of a private lender*. Let's begin...

Part 1: Predisposed

The first part of the Raising Private Money Formula is **Predisposed.** By predisposed, we mean concentrate on predisposed sources of private money - people who already have demonstrated their interest in investing in real estate.

Keep in mind, there are three things that need to be simultaneously sold when raising private money: 1) the merits of real estate as an asset class, 2) the merits of our particular deal and 3) our self. So by targeting predisposed sources, we have automatically reduced the sales effort by one-third. We don't have to sell predisposed sources on the merits of real estate. They already understand.

Targeting predisposed sources means that going to your favorite Uncle Teddy who rents his home may not be the best source. Or giving luncheons to dentists and doctors may not be the easiest place to start. Yes, dentists and doctors may have funds to invest *in something* but they may or may not be predisposed to invest in real estate.

Where do we find predisposed investors? Here's a partial list:

- Seller
- Self-Directed IRA Holders
- 1031 Exchangers
- Buyers at Real Estate Auctions
- Real Estate Clubs

- Past Sellers
- Past Brokers
- CPA and Attorney Referrals
- Friends and Family
- Hedge Funds
- Social Media

Personally, with just the first two (Seller and Self-Directed IRA Holders), you can fund all of the small commercial properties you'll ever want to do. It will certainly get you started. At least, that's what I did.

Seller

I place the Seller at the top of the list of predisposed sources because in any real estate transaction, there is no one more predisposed to seeing the deal get done than the seller. So, how can the seller be a source of funding for your deal? By seller financing - where they can take some or all of their purchase price in the form of installment payments, rather than up-front cash.

In the world of apartments, seller financing is quite common. Your seller will likely already understand seller financing. They've probably purchased property using seller financing. In fact, they expect you to at least *ask* about seller financing. That's why on every offer I and my students make we have at least two options that include seller financing.

Another way that the seller can be a source of financing is the fact that about half of all apartment mortgages, especially for mid-size and larger deals, are assumable. Always ask if their mortgage is assumable.

Bank Financing - Recourse vs. Non-Recourse

On the subject of assumable mortgages, let's talk about bank financing. In commercial apartments, there are *recourse* loans and *non-recourse* loans. Recourse loans are loans where there is a personal guarantor to the loan. In the event of default on the loan, the bank can take the property as well as pursue the guarantor for repayment of the debt.

Non-recourse loans are loans where there is no personal guarantor; the only collateral or security for the loan is the real estate. In the event of default, the bank can only take the real estate. Interestingly, non-recourse loans are only available for larger loans, generally $2 million and above.

With commercial real estate financing, the loan will be amortized over 15-30 years but there will generally be a "balloon payment" due within three to five years, usually five years. That means that although the loan payment may be calculated on a 25 year amortization, the bank requires that the loan balance must be paid off within five years. This is unlike residential where there is no balloon and you can have the entire amortization period to pay.

The most common ways of satisfying the balloon payment are to sell the property or refinance the property with a new loan within the balloon period. Let's get back to finding predisposed sources of private funding.

Self-Directed IRA Holders (OPI)

If you could choose only one source of private financing for small commercial properties (other than the seller), *this is the one*. You can buy property using other people's IRA's (OPI). The IRS allows anyone with a self-directed IRA to invest their retirement funds in your real estate project and earn a return which is tax-deferred or tax free.

Today, there is nearly $5 Trillion invested in IRA's and a good portion of that is self-directed; 97% of it earns less than 1% interest because the money is socked away in cash, money markets and CD's. The 2008-2009 market melt-down left those self-directed IRA holders very reluctant to return to the stock market. Those investors are *nationwide* and looking for solid investments where

114

they can earn above the 1% they are earning now. And they are being educated by the custodial accounts, which hold their monies, to invest in real estate. They just need a project to invest in – your project.

As a result, nationwide, there are actual networking events where self-directed IRA holders network with real estate entrepreneurs who have deals. It's the classic case of money looking for deals and deals looking for money. To find such networking events in your area, check with your local real estate investment club (always start there – it's an invaluable resource). Or you can check MeetUp.com. The IRA custodial companies (such as Quest IRA, Equity Trust, Entrust, Mid-Atlantic IRA) generally host monthly mixers as well.

Don't have such a networking group? Consider starting one. Think about it. If you want to be at the epicenter of private money in your area, start a private money networking club where predisposed sources of private money network with real estate entrepreneurs looking for deals. Your name will be associated with all private money deals. This single strategy could be huge for you.

Bonus Resource
Webinar: *How to Invest in Real Estate Using IRA's*
www.BMSABook.com/ira

1031 Exchangers

Another great predisposed source of private money is 1031 Exchangers; 1031 Exchangers are people who are selling real estate and they want to keep the profits tax-deferred by buying another piece of real estate within 6 months. But they have to declare the property they intend to purchase within 45 days.

It's very much a process of coordinating the sale of their property with the acquisition of your property. Well, this is perhaps the ideal predisposed source – someone that is looking to buy real estate and is working on a deadline. It's great for finding buyers on your wholesale deals.

Looking for an investor and not a buyer for your deal? Consider this. Have a 1031 Exchanger buy your property and you then buy it back from them under a lease-option.

Next, let's look at how to find large groups of buyers and predisposed investors in one location.

Buyers at Real Estate Auctions

Here's an easy one - your local real estate foreclosure auctions. Clearly, there you'll find predisposed sources of private money interested in real estate. How do we know they have the cash? Because it's cash on the barrel head at these types of auctions.

How do you get access? Well, how about handing out flyers announcing that you have great real estate deals looking for buyers and asking people to fill in their name, email and phone to be added to your buyers list. Some of those buyers might be just as happy as lenders. Or, again, maybe some of those buyers would be willing to buy the property and lease-option it back to you.

Can't make the auction? Send someone in your place to hand-out flyers for you and collect contact information. You can be doing this strategy in multiple cities as your commercial buyers and investors are not limited to your own back yard.

Here's another source of predisposed investors under your very nose.

Real Estate Clubs

This business is all about networking. If you are not a member of a local real estate club, join one. They are invaluable for your mindset in being surrounded by like-minded entrepreneurs. You'll stay afresh of the business and you'll meet private investors and buyers. There are people there with money who are obviously interested in real estate but don't have the time (or mindset) to find deals. As a newbie, I met my first two private investors at my real estate club.

Past Sellers

Once you do your first wholesale deal, you should immediately ask your seller what they intend to do with their cash. They are a predisposed source. You could direct them as a buyer or investor into your next real estate project. You could even 1031 exchange them into a project you have in the wings waiting to close.

If you've done several wholesale deals, go back to the sellers whom you have a relationship with and ask them if they'd like to invest in a small apartment project.

Now let's look at *referral sources* you can tap for accessing their network of predisposed investors.

Past Brokers

As part of marketing for deals, you are developing lots of broker relationships. What do brokers have access to? Buyers and investors. Leverage your broker contacts to find dollars for your deals. Of course, you have to pay them a commission when they refer you a buyer.

CPA and Attorney Referrals

CPA's and attorneys who specialize in real estate have clients who invest in real estate. They could provide you referrals to buyers or predisposed investors. How do you find CPA's and attorneys who specialize in real estate? Check the real estate clubs. They are congregating and advertising there because they are seeking real estate clients.

Friends and Family

Friends and family can help you find a predisposed investor by two ways: investing themselves or by leveraging their network. You want to approach them by asking, *"Who do you know who would be interested in earning an above market return investing in a small apartment project secured by real estate?"* They could answer, *"Me,"* or they could know someone. Think of all of the possible investors you could access by tapping into other people's networks. Have friends and family spread the word for you at their work place, church or temple, professional associations, school functions, etc.

Hedge Funds

As you get larger, ultimately you are going to be promoting to hedge funds, pension funds and REITs (real estate investment trusts). Hedge funds are basically private funds where a group of high net worth individuals pool their funds and hire a hedge fund manager to invest their monies. Hedge funds are for larger deals, looking to invest no less than $3 million upwards to $300 million. A little bit later, I'll share my conversation with a company that does this and how they structure their deals.

Social Media

This business is all about networking and the Internet, through social media, has given you the ability to network massively from your desk or phone. Social media outlets such as LinkedIn allow you to ask, *"Who do you know who would be interested in buying a small apartment project with an above market cap rate?"*

Case Study – Contractor Makes Perfect Investing Source

Recall Denon Williams and Terry Warren – my $6 Million men. Here's an example of how they funded one of their projects - the rehab and start-up of a mixed use project. They purchased a vacant building to convert to apartments and small retail shops.

They needed the down payment and financing for both the acquisition and rehab of the building.

To find a private investor, they asked a powerful question, *"Who would benefit more than me with a successful project?"* After all, if they could identify someone to benefit from their success, they'd have a predisposed source. The answer: their sheetrock contractor. Their sheetrock contractor agreed to put up the down payment and his credit as the guarantor of the construction loan. How did he benefit?

First, he became a partner in the project, receiving equity in the deal to share in the cash flow and forced appreciation. Second, he received the sheetrock contract for his business. Part of the loan proceeds came directly back to him as revenue to his business.

On every project you're looking to get funded, you want to always ask, *"Who would benefit more than me with a successful project?"*

Exercise: Find a quiet spot. Take 60 seconds and write down all of the predisposed sources of private money that you can think of. (Hint: Don't limit your brainstorming to who you know. Just concentrate on all of the places where predisposed sources can be found for your deals. Money follows deals. Don't forget about referrals).

That covers the first part. What's the second part of the Raising Private Money Formula? Actually, the second and third parts of the formula are related. Let's look at them.

Part 2: Control

Think back to a moment when someone asked you to borrow some money. Was your immediate thought, *"Gee, I wonder how much money I'll make?"* Or was it, *"Gee, I wonder if I'll get my money back?"*

For most people, it's the latter – *"Will I get my money back?"* Well, that's the mindset of every person that you approach in raising private money. It's the natural human reaction – and is wealth psychology at work. People's first concern is preserving their capital; they will think about this way before they get excited about increasing their capital.

A self-directed IRA investor said it this way, *"Tell me about return OF my capital before you tell me about return ON my capital."* And the rest of the Raising Private Money Formula addresses this basic human psychology.

The second part of the formula is **Control.**

Private money sources want to know how they can get control if you don't perform. So you want to show how they will have control. Acknowledge and concede their concern up-front. Show that you are pro-actively addressing their concern. This single act of addressing their concerns (up-front) will distinguish you from the herd.

Build control into your deal for your private money sources. Banks do it with a mortgage, which is simply a document that records the borrower's *obligations* and the lender's *remedies* in the event of default. These remedies include foreclosure and taking the property back so that they can sell it and get their money back.

And that is one of the beauties of real estate. With real estate, you have a hard asset that serves as collateral – the land and buildings. Now the value of that hard asset can also be dependent on how well you run it. That's why banks on apartment projects ask to see financials each year. And they retain the right to step in if the property is not performing – even if you are paying. They retain control. You can offer the same to your private investors.

Control also means such things as the private investor never releases their money until some promised event has occurred. For example, they only release the 20% down payment to an escrow officer at a closing – not to you directly.

Or they only release the rehab monies after the work is verified complete. That's how hard money lenders retain control – they use a first lien mortgage with controlled release of the monies. And they use *their* inspector to validate the work has been done properly (and they make *us* pay for the cost of their inspector).

Ever wondered why hard money lenders are able to loan cash so quickly on real estate deals? Well, part of the answer is that they structure their deals such that they retain pretty much *total* control. It's all stacked in their favor as the private money source.

Want to display even more control for your private investor? Well, rather than using a standard lien that requires foreclosure in the event of default, why not add language to your security agreement that allows the private investor to simply intervene in the project if you are more than 45 days late. Build in *easier* control for them in the event of default.

Show private money sources how they retain control and how you address their capital preservation concerns and you will become a private money magnet.

Exercise: Find another quiet spot. Take 60 seconds and write down all of the ways of building control into your private money transactions. (Hint: How do hard money lenders do it?)

Part 3: Low-Risk

Recall that both the second and third parts of the Raising Private Money Formula deal with the wealth psychology around preservation of capital, i.e. *"Tell me first about return OF my capital before return ON my capital."*

Well, the third and complementary part of the Raising Private Money Formula is **Low-Risk**. Low-risk means that the private investors feel that their investment is secure.

As an aside, this is why it was so enlightening for me to learn the techniques for buying businesses nothing down. Businesses generally don't have the same hard asset collateral as real estate. So learning the low-risk part of the Raising Private Money Formula for buying a business nothing-down presented me new techniques that may be applied to real estate. And you can apply them as well.

I think some Case Studies will best demonstrate what I mean by low risk.

Case Study – Mitigated Risk Hooks Investors, Raises $250,000

Here's an example of a 50-unit apartment I purchased. This is how I built in control and low risk in funding this deal.

The property's purchase price was $1.25 million – a good deal as it was appraised at $1.4 million. The bank was putting up a first mortgage of $1 million so I needed $250,000 cash down payment - to be raised through private money. I presented the deal to a family of three investors with self-directed IRAs.

Upon my initial inquiry, they expressed interest, *"Lance, it looks like an interesting project. We have one question. Who's going to run the project?"*

I explained, *"I am. It's a simple project; the property has high occupancy and it doesn't need any rehab. It's just a take-over. I'll choose and oversee the management company. I'll be the Asset Manager."*

They said, *"Great. We have confidence in you but we have another question. What if, God forbid, you're hit by a bus? Are we left with a 50-unit apartment building that we know nothing about?"*

Observe that their first question was about risk, not return. I prepared for it with the Raising Private Money Formula, so I used that opportunity to present how I was structuring the deal to provide them low risk and control, *"No, you won't be left with an apartment building. Let me tell you how I am protecting your money and how I've mitigated the risk - how I've made this a low-risk investment for you."*

"The first thing I'm doing is I'm buying key man life insurance – a life insurance policy which insures my life and names me as the key man for this project. In the event of my death, the life insurance policy is going to pay off the LLC which owns the property, and the LLC is pre-instructed to pay off the private investors."

They checked the box on that risk element. They liked that.

But then I went on, *"That's not all I've done. Of course, I'm obtaining casualty insurance - full replacement value coverage - so if one of my six buildings out there burns down, the casualty insurance will pay completely for its reconstruction even if the building codes have* changed. *Casualty insurance will completely rebuild that building. You won't need to put in future cash."*

I checked the box on that additional risk element. They liked that. And I continued.

"But that's not all. If one of the six buildings burns down, we'll have funds to rebuild it but that may take 6-8 months. In the meantime, I've lost one-sixth of my revenue because the residents had to move out and the new building is under construction. So to protect us during that time period of reconstruction, I'm purchasing business income loss insurance, which protects us in the event we lose revenue due to a casualty. The business income loss insurance will pay us for that lost rent revenue, so I can keep paying the taxes, the insurance, etc. And I can keep paying you."

They liked that a lot, too. And through the process, I continued to stack up all of the risk mitigating strategies that I was building into the transaction to provide them a low risk investment.

Finally, I said, *"And at all times, you're going to have control over your investment. You will have a collateralized lien – a lien which is recorded against the asset. That lien document has 2 parts: my obligations as the borrower and your remedies as the lender. In the event that I don't perform to meet my obligations, if there's a default of any kind, you're going to be able to exercise the remedies in that lien so that you can take control. Some of the remedies include replacing me as the manager of the LLC, changing the management company, and/or taking the property back to sell if I don't perform."*

That's what I mean by control and low risk and that's how I raised $250,000 cash on this transaction.

Management Experience

Let me add one more item that's important for low risk. New entrepreneurs will often ask me, *"I'm new and have no experience with apartments. Why would someone invest with me?"*

Management team experience is important. Just as in a business, banks and prudent private investors are going to look at the strength of the management *team* in assessing the risk exposure to their investment. They will typically ask who will manage the property or project. But it's important to realize that it's not a question of *your* experience, it's a question of your management *team's* performance.

So don't fret if you are new and don't have a strong resume yet. Remember, the definition of an entrepreneur is *someone who pursues his or her vision using the time, talents and resources (i.e. money) of others.* You just need to use the talents and resources of others. Bring on a partner and borrow *their* resume. It's common in multifamily projects to use the resume of the property management company to satisfy the experience requirement. You just need to adopt the attitude that as the entrepreneur, you are the matchmaker bringing together all of the components.

Case Study – Newbie Pitches a Hedge Fund Manager

Jim Craig got started with apartments where his prior experience in real estate was owning his own home. On one of his first projects, he put together a 7-figure portfolio deal to purchase. He arranged to present it to a Wall Street Hedge Fund Manager (remember hedge funds only do large deals). During his phone presentation to the hedge fund manager, he was asked, *"Jim, what is your experience in apartments?"*

Jim was prepared. He had assembled a top-notch team of an experienced real estate attorney and a marquee property management company. Jim replied, *"Here's my experience. Let me show you my team."* Jim reviewed the resumes of his experienced team members with the resulting comment from the hedge fund manager, *"You have good experience."*

Now, again, I'm *not* advocating that you pursue an elephant deal like this as your first entry. I want you to start small. But I do want you to adopt the same confident and *entrepreneurial attitude* that Jim displayed.

Bonus Resource
Webinar: *How to Present to Private Investors*
www.BMSABook.com/present

Better than Low-Risk

But let me come back to the risk with a final point... I have borrowed another technique that I learned from marketing genius, Jay Abraham. Jay Abraham always teaches about risk-reversal; the guarantee. Well, the ultimate risk-reversal is when the Lender actually benefits *more* if the Borrower defaults.

Say what?

Think about it. That's what hard money lenders do. They have a 65% LTV (loan-to-value) position and they get points (fees) paid up-front. If the borrower defaults, the hard money lenders actually make more money than if the borrower performs. That's another reason why they are willing to provide cash quickly.

In the event of default, the property's equity less the hard money lender's foreclosure costs still makes for a nice return. And because they use their own inspectors before releasing rehab monies, they retain control with no risk. They also mitigate the risk of loss by making the borrower pay for the insurance policy if there's a fire. You can adopt that same ***better-than-risk-free*** approach in structuring your private money transactions.

Exercise: Find a quiet spot. Take 60 seconds and write down all of the areas of risk in a real estate transaction. Take another 60 seconds and write down the ways to mitigate each of those risks. (Hint: Consider how banks mitigate their risks. Consider how hard money lenders mitigate their risks. Consider all of the things that we take for granted in risk mitigation – such as insurance – and consider which risk areas they mitigate.)

Now, let's review the last part of the Raising Private Money Formula.

Part 4: High-Return

So far, we've looked for people that are predisposed to real estate investing and we have shown how they can preserve their capital by building in control and low risk. Now once they are satisfied with that, the human greed factor kicks in and they want to see a high return. They are now ready to hear about *return ON their capital*. And that's the fourth element of the formula: **High Return**.

We want to offer an *above market* return but not give away the farm. We want to demonstrate a high return *relative to the low-risk investment* we have structured. More on this in a moment.

There are three ways, or models, to structure private money deals in generating investor return:

- **Model #1**: Lenders
- **Model #2**: Equity Partners
- **Model #3**: Hybrids

Model #1: Lenders

Lenders are going to loan you money for an interest rate return on their investment. This is my preferred investor return model. My private investors are lenders to my deal. I retain 100% ownership. This works well for stable projects that may require modest improvements.

Model #2: Equity Partner Model

Equity partners will put up all of the cash for equity or partial ownership of the deal, and you run the project. They will want control over the property but it is a good combination of leveraging their money and your time. It costs more – typically 50% of the cash flow and appreciation, in exchange for 100% of the capital. But it is a way to raise monies to do more deals; 50% equity will generally raise you all of the money you'll ever need.

However, an important point is that you *don't* have to give away 50% equity - it varies with the investor's return expectations.

Model #3: Hybrids

The *hybrid* return model is a combination lender and equity structure where maybe you pay 4% interest and give up 25% equity. Now I'm just throwing out numbers. Obviously, it will vary with the type of deal and you want to package it such that you retain a fair amount for yourself.

I know that deal structures is an area that everyone is especially interested in – what do the actual deals look like? Well, let me give you three examples.

Example #1: On an apartment project, the private investors are lenders that put up all of the cash (the down payment) and earn 10% APR. But in order to preserve the cash flow of the property, 4% APR is paid monthly and the other 6% APR is *deferred* and *accrued* until the private investors are paid off. This grants a nice future return to them and cash flow today to the entrepreneur. This type of model works when you have a plan to raise the property value through forced appreciation so that you have adequate equity to refinance and pay-off your private investors from the new loan.

Example #2: A local apartment rehabber takes really distressed properties (i.e. vacant) and revitalizes them back to stabilized operation. The high return they offer for their capital is usually 20% on the money. They employ the hybrid structure where they pay 7% interest guaranteed AND the private investor gets a 10-25% equity stake in the deal. The equity stake is set on the expectations of what it takes to generate an overall return of 20% on the private investor's money.

Example #3: Years ago, I had the opportunity to spend two hours with the owner of a national luxury apartment developer. They constructed thousands of apartment units nationwide. Their private investors were pension funds. They raised hundreds of millions of dollars. They utilized a hybrid model - paying 10% interest guaranteed and giving up to 50% of the equity. Now you might say that's a lot, but if you had access to $100 million, how much of the deal would you need to make a fortune?

A key part of this is to keep in mind the concept of cash flow and deferred interest payments. Recall that Example 1 had deferred interest payments for a portion of the deal. *All* of the interest could have been deferred and accrued. *Cash flow* to you is often the largest consideration in private financing – especially if you are acquiring apartments to become financially free and *passive income* is more important to you than equity. The beauty is that you can address it thru the three return models.

Exercise: Find a quiet spot. Assume you have a large rehab project on a vacant income-producing property that will take at least 6 months to rehab. How could each of the 3 deal models be applied to eliminate any out-of-pocket expenses from you as the entrepreneur?

Now, here's the real power behind the Raising Private Money Formula. Once you go to a predisposed source and put together a package that has low risk and the investor retains an element of control, now you are in a much stronger position to negotiate a win-win scenario, i.e. not have to give away the farm on the return. You want to spend a significant amount of time structuring the deal to minimize the risk: *the lower the risk, the lower the return expectation by the private investor.*

Don't Act Like the Amateurs

Most amateurs approach it from the other direction. They may just offer a high *absolute* return with the belief that a high return will make it easier to raise the money they need. Well, that may backfire on you. Let me ask you. What is the immediate connection you make with a high return investment offering, especially if it is not preceded by a conversation about the control and low risk? Answer: High risk.

And hence, promoting a high return as the sole feature of your deal may eliminate a large portion of your target private money group because the formula was not properly applied.

On the other hand, when you focus your efforts on first targeting predisposed sources and simultaneously building in control and designing a low-risk transaction, you can then promote an above market return to even a risk-adverse audience. You have demonstrated a consideration of their interests first and this pre-eminent approach is what attracts private money sources for life.

Case Study – Private Investors Nod Yes to This Formula

Let me return to my $6 million men, Denon Williams and Terry Warren. Recall they are the two business partners who funded $6 million of real estate purchases in 10 months – with none of their own cash or credit and with no prior experience. Denon and Terry assembled a group of entrepreneurs and investors and invited me to speak to the group on apartments. In that presentation, I shared this Raising Private Money Formula. At the end, Denon asked if he could come up and say a few words.

Denon explained to the group how he and Terry had funded their real estate deals using exactly this formula. He held up an Executive Summary and explained how they presented their deals to the investors thru the lens of the Raising Private Money Formula. Unbeknownst to me, Denon had a couple of his private investors in the room and he turned to them and said, "*Do you recall how we structured and presented the deal to you so that you first saw how you had control and low risk?*" They nodded yes. "*Do you recall how we offered you a high return relative to the low risk?*" They nodded yes again. Finally, Denon said, "*And do you recall how it worked with you?*" Again, they nodded yes.

That's the power of the Raising Private Money Formula. It inherently speaks to the psychology of the private investor. You structure and present your deals through the formula. The Raising Private Money Formula does the bulk of the work for you, even when you have no experience.

Here's one final example to make the point you are qualified to start raising funds today, even with no experience.

Case Study – Newbie Pitches Seller Financing to Veteran

Alan Cain was a newbie apartment entrepreneur with no prior experience. On one of his first deals, he sat down with an apartment owner to propose his seller financing offer. Now, this owner had owned his property for 20 years – he was a veteran of real estate. Alan was understandably nervous but he utilized the Raising Private Money Formula to structure his seller financing offer.

With the owner, Alan methodically presented – one by one - all the ways he had structured the deal to offer control and low risk to protect the investor, in this case the seller. At the end of the presentation, the seller exclaimed, *"Wow, you've taught me things that I didn't know. You really know your stuff. How long have you been doing real estate?"* Alan sheepishly admitted, *"Uh, this is my first deal."*

Become a student of and creatively apply the Raising Private Money Formula and you'll have all of the private money you'll ever need for your deals. In fact, use this 4-part formula to raise any resource you need for your project. But first, you must become a student of the formula.

SEC Guidelines

Before concluding this training, I need to say a few words about the Securities and Exchange Commission (SEC). The SEC was formed decades ago to protect small investors when making investments. It arose out of the abuses of a few unscrupulous deal makers in swindling small investors out of their money thru false promises and other shady methods. Note it applies only to raising private investors and NOT buyers, where you are simply wholesaling your contract.

This is a big topic and a separate training all in itself by securities attorneys. So let me first declare that <u>I am not an attorney and I am not giving legal advice</u>. There are securities laws and guidelines at both the individual state and federal level that form the boundaries of the playing field where we can operate when raising money from small investors. However, from my years, there is one thing that stands out for me with respect to understanding how to operate *well within the boundaries*.

That one thing is that you are free to raise private money from individual small investors with whom you already have a *relationship* with. And that's why I want you out networking – for all of the skillset and mindset benefits of being surrounded by like-minded people, but also for developing relationships with people who could be your next private money investor. Network at the real estate clubs, the self-directed IRA mixers, your professional associations – the other places I've been teaching you.

Do NOT go run ads in the newspaper or send out mailers which solicit investments from people you don't know. Just focus on the people whom you know, or develop new relationships, to do private money transactions. Remember that when you start with small apartments, you generally only need one person as your private investor – maybe that one person with a self-directed IRA with $50,000 to a few hundred thousand dollars. And the referrals from that initial successful investment can yield you all the money you need.

Coming Up...

In the next chapter, you are going to learn the five ways of getting started in apartments – of any size (small, mid-size or large). Then I'm going to reveal - for the first time outside of my paid boot camps - the 16 Strategies that I developed which are unique to small apartments. These strategies are what enabled me to leave the rat race. In fact, just one of the 16 strategies will allow you to do it.

Chapter Summary

- You are always marketing for two things: *deals and dollars*; this chapter is about the dollars, specifically the private investors who will fund your purchases or put up the credit.

- There is a four-part Raising Private Money Formula:
    1. Predisposed
    2. Control
    3. Low Risk
    4. High Return

- The same formula applies whether you are raising $6,000 or $6,000,000.

- The top two predisposed sources of private financing for small apartments are *"seller financing"* and *"self-directed IRA holders."*

- Seller financing is common with commercial real estate and especially small apartments.

- Another advantage of small apartments is that you don't need much (if any) cash to buy them; the private financing is simpler than mid-size and large. A single small investor is generally all you need as the seed to get you started.

- The investor cares about *"return OF capital before return ON capital."* The formula structures the deal with Control and Low Risk to address this.

- Use your property management company's resume as your experience when funding your first apartment deal.

- Offer returns that are high *relative* to the low risk. Don't offer high absolute returns.

- There are three types of Return models:
  1. Lender
  2. Equity Partner
  3. Hybrid
- Present your deal thru the structure of the Raising Private Money Formula; it positions you as knowledgeable and credible.
- Become a student of the formula. Use it to raise any resource you need.
- There are SEC guidelines and laws when it comes to raising private money. Stay well within the boundaries by focusing only on those individuals with whom you know or develop a relationship with.

Bonus Resources Summary

Webinar: *How to Raise Huge Money in Today's Economy*
www.BMSABook.com/rpm

Webinar: *How to Invest in Real Estate Using IRA's*
www.BMSABook.com/ira

Webinar: *How to Present to Private Investors*
www.BMSABook.com/present

Chapter 8

Five Ways to Get Started

W e've covered how to find the deals and how to find the dollars. Now, let's talk about how to monetize the deals. No matter the size of the apartment - small, mid-size or large - there are five ways to get started in this business:

- **Method #1**: Birddog
- **Method #2**: Wholesaling
- **Method #3**: Buy and Hold (Active Participant)
- **Method #4**: Buy and Hold (Passive Participant)
- **Method #5**: Rehab and Turnaround Distressed Apartments.

Method #1: Birddog

Let me tell you, up-front, I've cited this in the list for completeness but I'm not a big advocate of bird-dogging. *Birddogs* find leads and refer those leads to buyers. Those buyers then analyze, negotiate, contract, and close the deal, upon which they earn a small to modest finder's fee.

Most people do it because they are trying to learn how to enter the business. There are just a couple of small problems with birddogging: 1) you are never sure you will get paid and 2) it can be *illegal*. There are exceptions to the rule but state laws generally dictate that you have to have a real estate license to accept a commission for matching sellers and buyers. In Texas, I've had two real estate attorneys tell me the paying of referral fees to unlicensed persons is illegal for BOTH the payer and payee. I'm not an attorney so check with your state's Property Code or your attorney.

But even despite the legality question, you have no control over the deal since you aren't part of the contract. You rely on the buyer to pay you outside of closing. Let's review a much better method, which has no legal challenges and you already know.

Method #2: Wholesaling

Wholesaling picks up from bird-dogging but it *does not require a real estate license*. Besides finding the lead, the wholesaler analyzes the property, makes an offer to purchase, negotiates it and signs a formal contract to purchase, with themselves as the buyer. But here's the important part. On every contract – in the portion at the top where it names the buyer, I write <u>Lance Edwards, *or Assigns*</u>. The "*or Assigns*" addition is critical. Those two words mean I can assign my contract to any entity prior to closing. *Any entity* can take my place as the buyer (a person, a land trust, an LLC, or a limited partnership, etc.) and close on the deal.

In wholesaling apartments, I simply assign my place on the contract as the buyer to a new End-Buyer and they pay me an *assignment fee*. I notify the title company that the contract has been assigned and that an assignment fee is due me at closing when the End-Buyer closes. That deal *will not close without me getting paid*. I'm paid "at the table" since it was my contract.

Now, recall that a real estate license is required to introduce sellers and buyers. That's not what wholesalers do. Wholesalers sell contracts. Your product is not the property but rather the *deal* you put together – a signed contract with an already agreed price, terms, timing, etc. Because you are selling a contract, and not property, no real estate license is required.

And because you are selling deals, your assignment fee is a function of how good a deal you put together. The sweeter the deal, the more you should charge. All of the Case Studies in this book have assignment fees of no less than $10,000, and that's what you should expect as fair compensation for the effort of delivering a packaged deal with a bow on it to an End-buyer. All of the work has been done except for the final due diligence.

You can wholesale any size apartment or commercial property using this technique – and no license is required.

So when comparing bird-dogging with wholesaling, I'd much rather you start with the latter. Wholesalers make a lot more money plus you control the process since it's your contract. Birddogs hope someone throws them a bone after the meal is over. And wholesaling is legal.

Bonus Resource
Webinar: *How to Wholesale Apartments*
www.BMSABook.com/flip

A Side Note on Contracting

Even if you aren't planning to wholesale a property but intend to buy and hold it, I still encourage you to add the two words, "or Assigns," next to your name in the contract. For example, your purchase contract should read, Buyer is [Your Name], or Assigns. You never take title to a property in your personal name – for liability reasons. You use a limited liability company (LLC) or Land Trust, with an LLC.

The LLC or Land Trust is formed after the property is under contract and just prior to closing. But because your purchase contract is assignable, you assign the contract from you personally to your new entity and the property closes with your new entity as the owner.

Bonus Resource
Report: *20 Reasons You Should Use an LLC for Real Estate*
www.BMSABook.com/20llc

Bonus Resource
Webinar: *The Hidden Power of LLC's*
www.BMSABook.com/llc

Bonus Resource
Webinar: *Land Trusts Made Simple*
www.BMSABook.com/trusts

Given that contracting technique, let's review the two ways you can benefit from starting with buy and holds – actively or passively.

Method #3: Buy and Hold (Active Participant)

Buy and Hold as an Active Participant is where you purchase deals for yourself. Being the *Active Participant* means that you find the deal, analyze, negotiate and place it under contract to purchase. You then raise the funds from private investors, close the deal, and choose the management company. You act as the Asset Manager and manage the managers.

In my parlance of entrepreneur versus investor, you are the *entrepreneur*. You find the deal, you find the dollars and you match-make. In apartments, it's also known as being a *syndicator*. This is how I first got started.

If you want to take a more passive route and have funds or credit to invest, you can participate by the next method.

Method #4: Buy and Hold (Passive Participant)

Buy and Hold as a Passive Participant means that you invest in *other people's deals* (OPD). You are the investor. The entrepreneur, or syndicator, finds and runs the project and you earn a passive return. You have zero involvement in the operation or performance of the property.

If you have self-directed IRA funds or other funds to invest, this is a great way to leverage your newly acquired knowledge of apartments in selecting good projects in which to invest. After all, Chapter 5 taught you how to analyze deals and Chapter 7 revealed how deals should be structured to protect private money. Use that teaching to ensure that your money is protected, and in good deals.

Also, keep in mind that you cannot invest your own self-directed IRA into buy and hold projects which you or your entities own. You can only invest your self-directed IRA funds in passive projects, which you do not oversee. So if you want to buy and hold *both actively and passively* using IRA funds, you'll need to invest your IRA monies in other people's deals, not your own deal. Of course, you can invest any of your own funds that are not self-directed directly into your own project.

That leads to the fifth method for getting started and this is one where fortunes can be made quickly. It's rehabs and turnarounds.

Method #5: Rehab and Turnaround Distressed Apartments

Rehab and Turnaround of Distressed Apartments is where huge net worth improvements are created through forced appreciation. You seek out *distressed properties* which are underperforming, as evidenced by low occupancy or low rents due to mismanagement, lack of capital, etc. This includes vacant properties. The real gold nuggets are the ones where little capital is required and it just needs better management or better marketing.

Remember, you are in the marketing business, not the real estate business. So besides marketing for deals and dollars, you are also marketing for *residents* in any buy and hold situation and certainly in turnarounds. The fastest way to boost the NOI and the equity in any property is by raising the occupancy.

Recall the ratios I taught you in Chapter 5: a 2% occupancy increase translates into a $1,200 per door equity increase for ALL doors. So if you have 20 units, with 50% occupancy, and you raise it to 80% occupancy, that is a *$360,000 equity increase*. Do this for 200 units and that's $3,600,000!

Of course, you have to price it and buy it on the basis of *actual occupancy* not Pro-Forma occupancy, as I taught you. Too many people get in trouble buying distressed properties on a pro-forma basis. If you are into rehabs of houses, you definitely need to check out apartments. You place your crew on one location, they punch out cookie-cutter improvements and you reposition the property with better marketing so that you quickly fill it up. It's great leverage of your rehab capabilities without having to do it house by house.

Bonus Resource
Webinar: *How to Be an Apartment Turnaround Specialist*
www.BMSABook.com/turn

Those are the five methods for getting started. However, are you limited to just doing one method? Of course not, you can do multiple methods simultaneously. In fact, don't make the mistake I made when I started out. Remember my mantra, *"Always be wholesaling."*

Always Be Wholesaling

When I began, I was singularly focused on Method #3 – buying and holding as the active participant. In the process of creating my deal flow, I would evaluate my deals solely on the basis of whether I wanted to keep it. If a deal was too small or too large or too ugly, I would throw that lead away, even if it was a good deal.

Fortunately, I woke up one day and said to myself, *"Hey dummy. Those deals you are throwing away may not meet your criteria but they may meet someone else's criteria. Wholesale the deals you don't want to keep to someone else who considers that deal the perfect deal for them."* So when the next two deals came across my desk, I placed them under contract and flipped them to make $50,000!

I flipped a triplex and made $13,000. I flipped a vacant and boarded-up 56 unit complex to rehabbers and made $37,000. Your business is *deals and dollars* and your business objective is to monetize every lead. So, that's why I say that you should *"Always be wholesaling."*

Recall the Free in Five Plan I taught you in Chapter 4: *Flip 1, Flip 1, Flip 1, Hold 1.* Cherry pick the deals you want to hang on to as you build-up your passive income portfolio and drive towards financial freedom. Flip the rest to generate 5-figure checks along the way to pay today's bills. Flipping can allow you to replace the active income of your job with the active income of *wholesaling.*

Whether small, mid-size or large, those are your methods for monetizing your deals. Yet, when I started out with small apartments, I discovered and developed 16 sub-strategies that can be employed within the niche of small apartments.

16 Small Apartment Strategies

There are 16 sub-strategies that embrace the five methods, yet are largely unique to small apartments. I developed these sub-strategies on the front lines of capitalism when I was starting out. I have never shared these strategies outside of my paid seminars and coaching students but I want to demonstrate how you can be successful in small apartments if you pick only one of these 16 strategies.

16 Small Apartment Strategies

1. Single Flip
2. Peas in a Pod
3. Heal and Profit
4. Dominate and Profit
5. Bad Apple
6. Gentrification Riches
7. Special Needs
8. Buy Acres & Sell Lots
9. Starving Crowd
10. Connect the Dots
11. Partner for Profit
12. Own Nothing, Control Everything
13. Uncle Sam
14. Polish the Diamond
15. Leverage and Velocity
16. Money Before the Sale

These 16 strategies cover the following financial objectives: *active income* (quick cash thru wholesaling), *passive income* (thru buy and hold) or *net worth creation* (thru forced appreciation).

Strategy #1: Single Flip

Wholesaling is the most basic strategy, in which one finds a deal, finds a buyer, and flips the contract. I've covered this in detail already in other parts the book so I won't dwell on the technique here. But remember, *"Always be wholesaling."*

Case Study – $13,750 Made Flipping an Apartment with Snakes

Scott Kodak, who has a habit of wandering into banks and asking about real estate deals, found a 16-unit apartment that also had two commercial retail units downstairs, one of which actually sold snakes and another that housed birds. The bank told him straight-out that they did not want the property. He put it under contract for $175,000. He knew that he wouldn't be able to sell on the snakes alone, so he searched the county records for recent buyers of small apartments in the area and found his End-buyer. He flipped his contract, making $13,750.

Bonus Resource
Interview: *$13,750 Made Flipping an Apartment with Snakes*
www.BMSABook.com/snakes

Strategy #2: Peas in a Pod

This strategy is one of my favorites and is actually how I got my start. It is unique to duplexes, triplexes and four-plexes and can be done anywhere in the country. You can select to even do this in other states, sight unseen. It's simple and powerful.

Across the country, there are neighborhoods where, instead of building houses, the developers built duplexes, triplexes, or four-plexes. Imagine a neighborhood where, street after street, there are identical triplexes. Each of these triplexes is *individually owned* by an investor – who may or may not live in the same city or state. Very rarely do they live in their own building. We call these neighborhoods *pods*. We call each building a *pea*. Hence the name "Peas in a Pod."

I think the best way to explain Peas in a Pod is to give you an example.

Case Study – Part-Time Flipper Makes $26,500 in 60 Days

Henry Serrano was a part-time house flipper making the standard $3,000-$5,000 per house contract he sold. He got a lead on a triplex at his real estate club and ended up putting it under contract to purchase with the intent to flip the contract. Now, this triplex was unique in that it was surrounded by other triplexes in the neighborhood – street after street of triplexes, each owned by a different owner. Henry had identified a *pod of triplexes*. Henry wanted to flip his contract so he needed to find a buyer.

Remember, you are in the marketing business; marketing for deals and dollars. Henry had a deal. Now, he needed to find a buyer. In a pod of triplexes, where might you find a buyer interested in buying your triplex? That's right, one of the fellow owners inside the neighborhood (pod).

So, to market his deal, Henry obtained the list of property owners. And let's say there were 100. He mailed out a letter to the other 99 owners that basically said, *"I have a triplex for sale in the neighborhood. Before I offer it publicly, I wanted to see if you'd like the first chance to buy it."* From that letter, he found his buyer (a pharmacy owner) and flipped his contract for $16,500 – more than triple the profit of a single house flip. (As an aside, recall in Chapter 1 that I taught you that one of the large buying groups of small apartments is small business owners. This is an example). Back to the story.

After closing, Henry then did something very smart and which I want you to do. He went back to his buyer and asked, *"Would you like some more triplexes?"* The pharmacy owner replied, *"Yes, bring me all you can find. In fact, I'll bring in some of my friends to buy as well. I don't have time to go out and find these."* Now Henry had a buyer of triplexes. In other words, he had dollars looking for deals.

Where do you think Henry might find sellers of triplexes? That's right, in the same pod. So Henry prepared a second letter which said, "*I'm buying triplexes. If you would be interested in selling your triplex, please call me.*" He mailed it to the 96 owners who hadn't responded to his first letter. Out of that second mailer, he found a second deal. He placed it under contract and flipped it for $10,000 to the same buyer. With both deals, he made $26,500 over 60 days.

Henry will proudly tell you he used zero dollars of his own money in getting started, other than the cost of letters and stamps. He has since gone on to do this *seven times* within the same pod.

Bonus Resource
Interview: *Part-Time Flipper Makes $26,500 in 60 Days*
www.BMSABook.com/peas

That is the power of Peas in a Pod. You can execute this strategy remotely in pods across the country all thru the power of direct mail. Do it across several pods within a local area and you can even cross-market.

That's not the only way you can make money with pods. Let me show you two other strategies. Before doing that, I need to explain that, these pods have *Property Owner Associations* just like single family communities. Each building owner pays monthly association fees that are used by the association to maintain the common grounds, the common lawn, the signs, and the pool. These Property Owner Associations are directed by a Board, comprised of a few owners or their delegates. The owners vote-in the Board members once per year.

However, unlike house neighborhoods where the residents are primarily *owner-occupants* and display pride of ownership, the occupants of pods are almost exclusively residents, or tenants. And this can lead to pods where there is not a pride of ownership, so property management is very important. But property management is the *owner's* responsibility not the association's; the association is not a property management company.

If you have 100 owners, you might have 75 different managers. That means 75 different levels of management varying from good to bad. And a few bad management companies or bad owners who don't care can lead to a condition where a few blemished buildings can drag down the curb appeal of the *entire* neighborhood. Once the curb appeal of a neighborhood begins to deteriorate, the rent rates and market comps for the pod start suffering.

It's this condition that leads to the next strategy, *"Heal and Profit."*

Strategy #3: Heal and Profit

Heal and Profit is a variation of Peas in the Pod. With this strategy, you are looking for pods that are sick - where some of the buildings look shabby and/or the units have been rented to bad tenants, etc. These bad peas might be affecting all owners' ability to rent or sustain occupancy. You want to heal the sickness by cutting out the bad peas so that you raise the value of the neighborhood and your property.

You start obtaining control of the bad peas in the pod by buying them or putting them under option to buy. You then reposition these single buildings and start raising the level of these bad peas, thereby forcing the marketability up across of the whole pod. You can then hold the properties yourself for cash flow and resell them in the future at the new higher market value. Or you can wholesale the bad properties to investors and they initiate Heal and Profit.

Now, you might be asking, *"Why doesn't the association do something?"* That's a great question and here's the reality. Recall that associations are directed by boards which are comprised of owner *volunteers*. They generally don't have the time to get involved with these property management issues; that's not their charter. And, yes, they can adopt rules for all owners, but if they are weak in enforcing them (which many are), it contributes to a situation in a pod where it's *"every owner for himself."*

Once things start to deteriorate and there's a weak board, it really initiates a negative spiral – I call it the *death spiral*. Let me explain the sequence. First, as with any rental property, owners pay their monthly expenses and mortgage out of the rent revenue. They didn't count on paying it out of their pocket and often they aren't even in a financial position to do that. And when individual owners lose revenue and are not able to pay all of their monthly costs out of their own pocket, what do you think is the first thing they stop paying? That's right, their monthly association fees stop first.

Those funds are needed to maintain the common grounds. Lacking the monthly funds to operate the neighborhood, the association is forced to cut-back on lawn care, or the pool – which now really decreases the marketability of the entire pod. Imagine a neighborhood where the playground is knee-high in uncut grass. What signal does that send to prospective renters or buyers? When the *paying owners* see that the *bad owners* aren't being held accountable by a weak board, resentment builds up and the association dues plummet, leading to a distressed pod and the death spiral. These associations are called *"fractured associations."*

Individual owners of fractured associations feel helpless and hopeless, other than shouting at annual Property Owner Association meetings. That's where you can step in and help with the strategy, *Dominate and Profit*.

Strategy #4: Dominate and Profit

First, let me say that this strategy is not for everybody – and probably not newbies. But even if you're a newbie, I want you to know it for future use after your first deal. It pays big because the challenge is bigger.

Dominate and Profit is a variation of Heal and Profit. Whereas in Heal and Profit, the objective is to heal a few bad peas for the sake of the pod, Dominate and Profit is used when massive action is required to save the pod. Someone needs to step in and take control. The inherent cause of the problem with fractured associations is in trying to reposition a distressed pod to *act* like one apartment complex where there may be 50 different owners. Imagine trying to turnaround a single 300 unit apartment complex where you need the agreement of 50 people on what to do (and you need all 50 to contribute financially). Good luck.

So, the objective is to obtain enough control (greater than 50% voting rights) to dominate the property owners' association and operate the pod *as a single large apartment community.* You want control because, with control, you can elect the Board. You can fairly easily become the Board (no one wants to do it) but you have to be prepared to act as a strong board and enforce the collection of association dues for the survival of the pod.

You obtain control by buying up the individual buildings (peas) or, even better, by getting options to buy individual peas from distressed owners (along with their proxy). Keep in mind, with a distressed pod, owners will follow just about anybody who has a reasonable plan. Once you have options on a majority – or most – of the peas in the pod, you insert a single management company that you control so that the individual buildings are operated like a *single apartment complex.*

It takes a lot of work and time. It's risky, capital intensive and it may take two years but the pay-off can be huge.

Case Study – Dominate and Profit Pays $5,000,000

Despite my own advice to you to the contrary, I started my real estate journey leading the charge on a Dominate and Profit strategy. I identified a distressed pod of fifty four-plexes and started buying. At the same time, there was a friendly competitor in the pod who was doing the same. He was improving his buildings and he was all about revitalizing the community; he and I actively sat on the board together. He even built his new office building right next to the pod so that he could keep an eye on things. Over a span of 18 months, he obtained control of virtually the entire pod except for my four-plexes. He and I mutually benefitted but he really wanted my buildings – I was the last hold-out. Guess who got the highest price ever paid for a four-plex in that neighborhood up to that time? That's right, yours truly.

Here's an update. My friendly competitor was paying about $135,000 per four-plex when he started his Dominate and Profit. He injected time and capital and inserted his own management company to manage ALL the units. He renamed the pod. He encircled the pod with an attractive wall and installed gated access. He transformed it into a very nice community of apartment <u>homes</u>. He created immense cash flow for himself. A few years later, I saw on MLS that he was selling the individual four-plexes for $235,000 to individual investor-owners. Recall he paid $135,000. Let's do the math. That's 50 buildings x $100,000 gross profit = $5,000,000 exit. Not bad.

Now, you're probably saying you don't have the time or the capital or the experience to Dominate and Profit but here's an alternative approach. You be the front-person. You approach the individual owners of a distressed pod and you place their building under option – with no guarantee other than your presentation of this Dominate and Profit plan. When you possess a sufficient number of options, you sell the bundle of options to a partner with the means (capital, time, experience) to do the execution.

This is how you can benefit from bad management; let me show you another way to benefit from bad property managers.

Strategy #5: Bad Apple

The Bad Apple Strategy is a technique for finding multiple distressed owners in a unique way: by following the trail of bad management companies and learning which properties they manage. If a management company manages one property poorly, there's a good chance there are others. And when you contact the clients of bad management companies, you will find motivated sellers.

You can find the bad management companies by utilizing a couple of methods. First, through your normal speaking with brokers and sellers, try to discern if there's any kind of distress due to poor management. Ask who does the management. This is a lead to a bad management company. Second, when you notice shabby properties in your own city, find out who's managing them. Often, there's a sign by the management company on the building. If there are "For Rent" signs, call them up. Once you identify a bad management company, you can find out what other properties they manage from their website, or by just calling and asking them. Follow this trail of breadcrumbs to find the motivated sellers.

Case Study – Bad Management Makes For a Good Deal

Jon Perry found a 42-unit building where the management company only collected the rent and did nothing else. The property had essentially been run into the ground. And the bank didn't want it. Jon placed it under contract at $5,000 per door and the bank agreed to finance it with only 5% down; he received 95% financing in exchange for a $10,000 down payment. Jon was used to rehabbing houses and so he expected to put $10,000 per door into the property in the form of rehab and carrying costs. Once stabilized, he estimated the resale value would be approximately $25,000 per door. Since his all-in price would be $15,000 per door ($5,000 +$10,000), he expected a gross profit of $10,000 per door, or $420,000.

Bonus Resource
Interview: *Bad Management Makes for a Good Deal*
www.BMSABook.com/rehab

Let's now look at a strategy for monetizing deals in *"good neighborhoods."*

Strategy #6: Gentrification Riches

Gentrification Riches is another variation of the Single Flip and Peas in a Pod. Gentrification is when old undesirable areas become desirable due to their proximity to new amenities or the revitalization of a nearby area. Gentrification is evidenced by the phenomenon of old houses being purchased for the purpose of tear-down and replacement with larger, more expensive homes. The value is in the land and location, and this is a ripe target area for flipping. When you find a property in an area of gentrification, you can flip to those who have recently moved to the area. They believe in the area's rising real estate values and they want more.

Case Study – $13,100 Flipping a Non Cash-Flowing Triplex

I had a contract on a triplex in an area of revitalization. The triplex was surrounded by old homes built in the '20s, and they were being bought and torn down in order to build newer homes – due to gentrification. Given the high demand for the area, I asked, *"Who would be predisposed to buy this triplex from me?"* The answer: other single family home residents within a couple of streets of the triplex.

I put together a simple letter which said, *"I am selling a triplex at 123 Smith Street and before I go public with the listing, I thought I'd give you first option to buy it. If interested, call me."* Sound familiar to the Peas in a Pod approach? I mailed it to home owners on the same street of my property and to the two streets on either side. The owner of a handsome new home, three houses down, contacted me and indicated his interest in buying for cash.

Side Lesson: Don't make my mistake. Once I had interest expressed by a buyer, I stopped my marketing. That was a dumb move because the buyer dallied around and then changed his mind. I ultimately found a local realtor who specialized in the area and found me a buyer. My profit was $13,100, and that was after paying the realtor. The lesson learned: *Don't stop marketing for your buyer until the deal closes*. Take back-up offers. When you have multiple buyer inquiries, add them to your buyer's list for the next deal.

Strategy #7: Special Needs

Special Needs is a buy-and-hold strategy solely focused on generating cash flow or equity thru forced appreciation. Here's the strategy: find a deal and buy it (using other people's money). But instead of just leasing to anyone, you focus on leasing to special needs groups which pay a premium rent. And with that premium rent comes higher NOI, higher cash flow and forced appreciation.

Special needs groups include any type of supportive housing, such as Section 8, transitional living, VA housing and other federally funded programs where the rent voucher amounts are specified by HUD and pay higher than "street rent." Special needs groups also include private-pay assisted living and student housing, which are booming niches.

You can even tailor your property to special needs groups and market directly to the agencies or organizations which will gladly refer the residents (and rent vouchers) to your apartments. Fit your product to their needs. Hardly anyone does this. How do I know? This is how I started out.

For example, many universities are experiencing housing shortages and will gladly advertise your small apartments for you. But here's the really cool part, the companies that do student housing *rent by the bed*. Last time I checked, one apartment solely dedicated to student housing near the University of Houston was getting $450 per bed, with *two* beds per room. That's $900 total rent on a one-bedroom and $1,800 on a two-bedroom. Of course, you have to offer the units as All Bills Paid and furnish them but they are cash cows.

You can do the same with Assisted Living; it's experiencing explosive growth due to the aging of the baby boomers.

Case Study – Special Needs Partnership Yields Cash Flow

Path to Independence (PATH) is a for-profit organization that provides transitional living to men coming out of substance abuse programs. These men need a safe, clean and sober environment as part of their rehabilitation. It's called *transitional living* and is a housing environment where men live under supervision for a short time period prior to going back out on their own. A house manager lives with them, their meals are provided, and they are given jobs by the group in order to pay their rent.

PATH rented by the bed, charging each man $100 per bed, per week. And PATH needed three-bedroom apartment units for their program. As you might imagine, they had challenges finding apartments willing to take them so they approached me, explained their program and what it meant to their clients. They showed me how I should not expect any trouble.

I gave them a shot and, as a special needs group which was *for-profit*, rented PATH a three-bedroom unit for $895, where the market rent was $720. They were the best residents I ever had; the units were always clean, nicely decorated and they were the quietest men you'd ever meet. I ended up leasing them every three-bedroom apartment we had – and gladly. As a matter of fact, I even helped them with their marketing to grow their business.

Let's look at another strategy for forced appreciation.

Strategy #8: Buy Acres and Sell Lots

Buy Acres and Sell Lots is a rehab strategy that is loosely similar to Special Needs. The term comes from the model where land developers buy land at price A, add basic improvements such as roads and utilities and then subdivide the land into lots. They then sell the individual lots at a premium; the total price for the sum of the lots is greater than the original price A, plus the improvement costs.

It's a powerful strategy for land and you can do the same with your apartments.

Case Study – Subdivided Building Becomes Cash Cow

Let's talk about Terry Warren and Denon Williams again. They purchased a 12-unit building made up of two bedroom units that were converted to three bedrooms. Instead of renting by the unit at $600 per month, they rented *by the bedroom* at $450 per month. With three-bedrooms per unit, they received the equivalent of $1,350 per unit.

Each resident (which were all men) shared the kitchen, bathroom and a small living room with a lock for their own bedroom. The units came furnished and it was All Bills Paid. The property was transformed into a cash cow because of its repositioning into smaller and marketable units. Their typical resident was a cross-country truck driver who was primarily on the road but needed a place to keep his belongings and a "crash pad" when he came home.

Other target markets for this type of housing include transient construction workers and even traveling salesmen. Student housing is an adaptation of Buy Acres and Sell Lots.

Let's now discuss Strategy #9, feeding the Starving Crowd.

Strategy #9: Starving Crowd

If you were trying to set up a restaurant, how do you know which type of food to offer? The answer: choose a food that *feeds the starving crowd*. Always build a business that matches the demand of the *buying mob*. It keeps things easy. And when it comes to finding buyers for small apartments, the starving crowd is single-family landlords – rental house owners who self-manage. Most operate with the false belief they need to graduate from single family to multifamily so show them how they can "move up to small apartments."

Single family landlords are easy to find and market to. They are at the real estate clubs. They are at the real estate auctions and they're easily accessible via direct mail. Just search for house owners who have a different mailing address than the property address or who don't claim a homestead exemption. Promote your small apartment as the *"Perfect Small Apartment Starter"* and put it in front of house landlords and watch them light up.

Case Study – Spoon-Feed the Starving Crowd

I was selling a 10-unit property and decided to promote it at my real estate club's monthly "Deal A Minute" session. If you're not familiar, it's when club members are given 60 seconds to stand in front of the room and offer their deals for sale. Being a real estate club, most of the members operated in single family and all of the 60 second presenters that preceded me had a house they were looking to flip. They talked in detail about the number of bedrooms, the ARV, the repair costs, etc. They cited a lot of numbers and from what I could observe lost most of the audience. Most went beyond their 60 seconds.

When my time came, I stood up-front and instead of taking 60 seconds, I spoke for maybe 8 seconds. I said, *"I have the perfect small apartment starter package. It's 10 income producing units in one. I have a flyer prepared with all the details and I'll be in the back of the room. Come see me."* Then I walked to the back of the room. Not once did I mention the price, the number of bedrooms, the rents. Nothing else.

I was mobbed. I guess there were 120 people in the room and at least 30 came back to grab my flyer. In speaking with them individually, I emphasized the headline on the top of the flyer which read, *"Perfect Small Apartment Starter Package. Buy 10 Income-Producing Units in One."* Most of them explained how they had been doing houses; how they were tired of self-managing and, as a result, they had been thinking about moving up to small apartments. In the end, they said, *"This looks perfect for me."*

Want to know who bought that 10 unit apartment? A single family landlord. Feed the *starving crowd*.

Your Buyer's List

When wholesaling, you can easily attract a large starving crowd when you market a small apartment. However, only one person can buy your property. And so here's how I observe most house wholesalers operating: they find a deal, they market it, they find a buyer. And then they start from scratch all over again. It pains me.

When I marketed the above 10 unit property, I not only showed it at the real estate club, I placed it on every listing service including MLS and LoopNet. But I didn't give all of the information away up-front. I set up my Buyer Generator *System* where every inquirer had to request information such that my *system* captured their *name, email address and phone number* 24/7. At the end of the day, there was only one buyer but 637 people asked for information. How do I know? Because my system collected every inquiry automatically and added it to my *buyer's list*.

Your buyer's list is a key asset for your business, which leads to the next strategy.

Strategy #10: Connect the Dots

Connect the Dots is how you escape the grind of starting every day from scratch. When you have a buyer's list that includes a name, email and cell phone number, you have direct access to a predisposed group of small apartment buyers. So, now when you have a deal to flip, you can notify them *first* via email, text, and voice message. You are *connecting deals and dollars* automatically. And every time you market a new property over Internet-based listing services, or via newspaper ads, real estate flyers, or auction flyers, you have another opportunity to add to your buyer's list. It's another way that you *leverage every activity* thru *systems*.

What if you are new and don't have a deal or a buyer's list? Here's a way to build your buyer's list even when you don't have your own deal. Approach a member of your real estate club that has a house deal and offer to joint venture with them to market their deal. But you get to keep all of the leads.

Set up a *Buyer Generator System* like I do and build a buyer's list of houses using OPD (other people's deals). Then when you do have a small apartment to flip, you connect the dots by putting your deal in front of your list. Remember, house buyers are the biggest starving crowd for small apartments.

That's how you leverage your marketing activities to find buyers (the *dollars*). Let me now show you how to leverage your marketing activities in finding the *deals*; by offering to partner.

Strategy #11: Partner for Profit

Partner for Profit is how you can find lots of off-market distressed apartment deals. This approach really boosts your direct mail response. Rather than sending a letter that says, "*I want to buy your property*," send one that says "I am willing to buy *or partner with you to improve* your property." Watch your inbound calls increase. Motivated sellers who have a problem with their property tend to be embarrassed and an offer to help is even more receptive than an offer to buy. If distressed owners can see a way to gracefully exit and save face, they are really interested in talking.

Of course, you have to be sincere in your offer to partner with them. And in the next strategy, I'll show you how. But here's an interesting observation: property owners may express interest initially in partnering but very few ever do. In the end, they decide they just want out – and they sell. However, the Partner for Profit approach is what gets them to initially call you.

Case Study – Hawaiian Property Owners Need Help

My very first marketing campaign was 50 letters to people who owned property in my home of Houston but lived in Honolulu, Hawaii. Why Honolulu? I was planning to vacation there within a few weeks and my idea was to meet with a few owners in Hawaii. After all, they were out-of-state landlords and might be motivated to sell.

I prepared a letter which essentially said, *"If you are dissatisfied with your Houston real estate investment, I would like to meet you in Honolulu on July 16. I am willing to buy or partner with you to improve your property."* Now, if you are familiar with direct mail, you know that a 1% response rate is a good response. Want to guess my response rate? Come on, guess. It was 30%!

Out of 50 letters, I met 15 people that day in Honolulu. From this group, I ultimately bought 23 *properties using none of my own cash*. Many expressed interest in partnering but none did. They all decided to sell. And that's how I got my start, by offering to help.

So let's next look at how you can structure partnership deals.

Strategy #12: Own Nothing, Control Everything

Own Nothing, Control Everything is a cash flow and forced appreciation strategy where you don't own the property but you *control* it. Once you learn it, you'll realize that control can be more powerful than ownership, with *less risk*. This strategy is an extension of Partner for Profit, where you offer to partner with owners to improve their property. Here, you'll learn a powerful way to structure the partnership deal. It's also a way to upright deals that are *upside down*, i.e. the property is worth less than the money owed the bank.

So, here's a scenario. From your marketing for deals, you come across this situation on a 20 unit small apartment: The owner lives out-of-state. He's been putting nothing back into his property for years. It needs $20,000 of rehab but he doesn't have it. It's looking shabby and the management company has been forced to lower the rents in an attempt to maintain occupancy. The property is slipping away with deferred maintenance and a lower quality tenant mix. As a result, the value has declined and it's now *upside down*; the owner owes more than it's worth. He can't sell it.

So you approach the owner with this proposition, "*I want to improve your property using my money.*" His response, "*How are you going to do that?*" Here's how you do it: a device called a *Master Lease Option,* combined with private money.

First, the owner gives you a five year lease on the property whereby you take over as the *Master Tenant* with the right to sublet to the existing tenants. You *control* the property. You choose the management company, you collect the rents and you pay all the bills including the mortgage. Depending on the situation, you keep most, if not all, of the cash flow. It's called a Triple Net (NNN) Lease and you control the property as if it's yours. The owner doesn't have to write another check or deal with it.

Second, in consideration of you taking on all the responsibility, the owner gives you a five year *option* to purchase the property at a price corresponding to today's mortgage balance of $350,000 plus 10% of the profit you create. (Remember the property is upside down, so its value is less than $350,000 due to the declined performance).

You've done your forced appreciation calculations like I taught you in Chapter 5 and you project that, after inserting $20,000 rehab and new management, you can raise the occupancy and rents so that the new retail value of the 20 units will be $550,000 – all within 18 months. The value of your option at that point is *$200,000* ($550,000 - $350,000).

But who pays the $20,000 for rehab? You show the deal to the investor you met at the self-directed IRA mixer and she agrees to invest $20,000 from her IRA.

Roll the calendar forward 18 months: The property is rehabbed and the new management company has boosted the rents and occupancy up to 90%. The NOI is up and the property appraises for $550,000. How do you exit? One way is you could hang on to it and buy out the owner within the next few years.

Or you could sell your option that's worth $200,000. You decide to cash-out so you sell the option at a discount for $150,000 cash - out of which you repay your private investor her $20,000 plus her return and you pay the owner $15,000 for being your partner. You net over $100,000 on a property which you didn't own, that required no bank financing and the $20,000 came from someone else.

Now do you see how control can be better than ownership? Let me now show you how Uncle Sam will also contribute to your wealth creation plan.

Strategy #13: Uncle Sam

The government, good ole Uncle Sam, has established a number of ways to assist you in creating wealth faster when you own investment real estate such as small apartments. It comes thru tax breaks that are fully sanctioned by the IRS, for both your appreciation and depreciation.

First, let me share how they allow you to keep your appreciation.

1031 Exchange

In Chapter 2, I explained a 1031 Exchange whereby you pay *no tax* on the profits from the sale of your real estate when you buy another piece of real estate within 6 months. There are some other simple guidelines, including you have to do it thru what's called a *1031 Exchange Intermediary*. There is no limit to the number of times you can do this and this is how you can start small and quickly ramp up to larger properties thru forced appreciation. I'll show you how in the next strategy, *Leverage and Velocity*. Here's another Uncle Sam tax benefit.

Owner-Occupant Tax Breaks

The IRS allows you to keep the cash from the sale of a property *tax free* when you occupy the property. So what does that mean for your small apartments? Well, if you live in one of the units of your four-plex, you can keep one-fourth of your profits *tax free* cash when you sell. You can do this every two years up to $250,000 as a single person and up to $500,000 if you're married. See your CPA.

Case Study – Owner-Occupant Lives Rent-Free

Let's move back to the Gentrification Riches Case Study of a triplex I flipped for $13,100 in a very desirable neighborhood. The buyer who ended up closing lived in a nearby apartment where she paid rent. She liked the area, so she bought the triplex with the intent to live in one of the units while leasing out the other two. She generated equity for herself and had her tenants paying the mortgage. When it comes time for her to move on, she can lean on Uncle Sam to keep one-third of her cash *tax free* when she sells - as long as she's lived there for two years.

Show buyers of your small apartments that they can be owner-occupants and benefit from Uncle Sam's tax strategies. Not only does Uncle Sam give us tax breaks on appreciation but he also does it for *depreciation*.

Depreciation Tax Breaks

Depreciation is a *paper loss* that is allowed on your tax returns. The IRS assumes real estate depreciates all of its value over 27.5 years. (In fact, it's actually appreciating so that's why it is a paper loss). I won't cover it here but there are techniques to depreciate certain components - like the appliances - at a much faster rate than 27.5 years. It's called *componentizing*.

As a simple math example, assume you own a building which you purchased for $2,750,000 (not including the land value). The

IRS figures that it is depreciating at the rate of $100,000 per year ($2,750,000 / 27.5 years). You can deduct that $100,000 per year paper loss from your job income, thereby lowering your total tax bill. There are caps on the paper loss you can take in a year *unless* you declare yourself a *real estate professional.*

It does not require you to have a license. The definition of a real estate professional for the IRS is someone who works 500 hours per year in real estate. That's 10 hours per week – which is probably your situation. See your CPA.

So, in this example, if you are a real estate professional and you make $75,000 per year in your job, you can offset all of that income with $75,000 of depreciation paper losses from investment property you own. You would pay no tax on your *active* income, which is the highest tax rate. You only pay income tax on the *passive* income of your property – a low tax rate.

Bonus Resource
Webinar: *Real Estate Tax Strategies Your CPA Doesn't Know*
www.BMSABook.com/taxes

Let's now look at a strategy for buying non-distressed *pretty* apartments.

Strategy #14: Polish the Diamond

Up to now, we've been talking about forced appreciation for underperforming properties where you can force the value up by raising the rents and/or occupancy. What if you find a property that's performing well? How do you buy it? You use *Polish the Diamond.*

When you find a property that is already performing well, your value play is to *buy it right* – meaning that you want to buy it at slightly higher cap rate than the market cap (lower price) or you buy it with flexible financing such as owner-financing. Here's the important rule. Do not overpay. Use the techniques I taught you in Chapter 5. Stick to the numbers.

Case Study – Polishing a Diamond

Kathy Blocher-McCabe found a 12-unit for sale through a broker. The owner had owned the property for years and had personally managed it. In fact, he had practically manicured it under his watch. It was 100% occupied with no deferred maintenance. There was no room to raise occupancy of course but it could probably stand some $10 rent increases. Kathy ran the numbers and it was way over-priced at the Ask Price. The owner was really proud of his small apartment.

Kathy stuck to the numbers and made an offer that was 33% below the Ask Price. They declined and Kathy simply told them, *"Keep me in mind if the situation changes."* She kept in touch and six months later, she got the call from the broker, *"Hey Kathy, are you still interested in that 12-unit?"* She came up just $4,000 from her original offer price and funded it with private money. Kathy stuck to her guns and "bought it right."

I've shown you numerous strategies for creating equity thru forced appreciation. Let me now overlay a super-strategy for amassing wealth quickly with apartments.

Strategy #15: Leverage and Velocity

I've shown you the power of *leverage* in buying apartments with OPM; now you'll learn how to increase the *velocity* of your wealth creation. Leverage is the ability to buy properties using other people's resources. Velocity is leveraging that equity and doing it over and over again. Make the numbers work for you.

Let's start with you buying an eight-unit small apartment for $200,000. You negotiate owner financing and you can buy it for 10% down, or $20,000. That's leverage.

• $20,000 Down payment → $200,000 apartment

You run your numbers and you conservatively estimate that you can raise the value 5% per year thru *forced appreciation*, or $10,000 per year. After two years, the value is increased $20,000.

• 5% Forced Appreciation → $20,000 equity (in 2 years)

At that two-year point, you refinance the property and pull your $20,000 of equity out and use it to buy a second eight-unit apartment building.

• Refinance and take-out $20,000 → Buy 2nd apartment

Continue to assume 5% forced appreciation but now it's on two apartments. After another two years, you refinance both properties and pull out $40,000. You use that as down payment to buy two more buildings. You now have four apartment buildings (eight-units each).

• Repeat: Buy third and fourth apartment buildings

You continue with 5% forced appreciation over four buildings and two years later, you refinance the four buildings to pull out $80,000 which you use as down payment to buy four more buildings. Now you have eight buildings.

• Repeat every two years → eight apartment buildings

If you run it out to seven years, those eight apartment buildings are now worth $2,100,000 and your equity is $270,000. That does *not* include the mortgage buy-down nor the cash flow received. You started with $20,000 cash and created a 13:1 return on the cash.

• $20,000 Cash → $270,000 equity after seven years

You use leverage to buy the properties. Velocity is taking that equity and pulling it out to reinvest again. That's *Leverage and Velocity*.

You might be saying, "*I don't have the $20,000 cash for a down payment.*" Okay, suppose you raise the $20,000 from a private investor and offer to split the equity gain 50/50 after the seven years. They'd get back $135,000 on their $20,000 investment; that's better than a 6:1 return. You keep the other $135,000 (Tip: Don't offer 50%, it's too much).

That's a small apartment example. Imagine repeating this example by adding a zero. Start with an 80 unit building for $2,000,000 and $200,000 cash down payment. After seven years, the equity is $2,700,000. Split that 50/50 and your share is $1,350,000.

That's why I say you should start small but *scale-up*. Now, this example was intentionally simplified for illustrative purposes. You'll need more down on some deals or maybe you'll need less on others. You'll generate more than 5% appreciation on some. You could jump from 8 units to 50 units. The point is to show you the power of *Leverage and Velocity*.

The previous 15 strategies should have you seeing the abundance of opportunity in monetizing your deal flow and leveraging every lead and every activity. Let's look at how you can make money before your first deal.

Strategy #16: Money Before the Sale

In *Connect the Dots*, I explained the power of having a buyer's list to quickly monetize your deal flow in flipping. I pointed out how your buyer's list is an asset. In fact, there's a saying in marketing, *"the money is in the list."*

Money before the Sale is another way that you can monetize your buyer's list without doing a real estate deal. What else can you sell them? What do real estate buyers crave besides real estate? I'll tell you; they crave *information* about real estate. You're an example. You have this book about how to do real estate.

So with your buyer's list, you have a starving crowd for *"how to"* information in real estate. You can sell them other people's information and earn commissions as an affiliate. You don't need a product, you don't need a website, you don't need a credit card processing account, and you don't need to do any selling. Besides your list, you don't need anything except the ability to send emails to your list (and the emails are written by the information product owners).

Here's how it works as an affiliate: you send an email advertising someone else's website or webinar. The product owner provides everything including the selling. And when your referral buys, you receive a commission check. That's it. You need to be doing this. You could use this strategy to pay for your direct mail campaigns or your phone bill or hiring a virtual assistant or the down payment on your next property.

What type of information do your buyers crave? Being also in the "how to" training business, I can tell you type of information real estate entrepreneurs crave:

✓ Entities & Asset Protection   ✓ Wholesaling
✓ Land Trusts   ✓ Asset Management
✓ Tax Strategies   ✓ Other Real Estate Niches
✓ Funding Deals   ✓ Etc.

As a reader of this book, you are invited to become an affiliate of my real estate information products and execute your own Money Before the Sale Strategy.

Bonus Resource
FREE: *Become an Affiliate of My Products*
www.BMSABook.com/affiliate

Those are your 16 small apartment strategies. As you can see, some are extensible to mid-size and large apartments. Remember, I recommend you start small to get that critical first apartment deal done and then you scale-up.

Coming Up...

In the next chapter, I explain what few others talk about in real estate: the four components of success that are essential to distinguishing you amongst the 5% in real estate who are making all of the money. Disregard this next chapter and you're at serious risk of being left out from those making the *real* money in real estate.

Chapter Summary

- There are five basic ways to get started in apartments, whether small, mid-size or large:
    1. Birddog
    2. Wholesaling
    3. Buy and Hold (active participant)
    4. Buy and Hold (passive participant)
    5. Rehabs and Turnarounds

- Bird-dogging generates the least money and is illegal in most states when done without a real estate license.

- Always Be Wholesaling – even if your primary strategy is to Buy and Hold.

- No license is required for wholesaling. You are not selling the property; you are selling a deal – your contract.

- Your buyer's list is an asset. Add to it with every deal you wholesale.

- *Flip 1, Flip 1, Flip1, Hold 1*: Cherry-pick the deals you want to hold on to, and flip the others to generate cash while building your portfolio.

- There are 16 small apartment strategies that I developed. Use these to begin and/or to scale-up.

16 Small Apartment Strategies

1.	Single Flip	9.	Starving Crowd
2.	Peas in a Pod	10.	Connect the Dots
3.	Heal and Profit	11.	Partner for Profit
4.	Dominate and Profit	12.	Own Nothing, Control Everything
5.	Bad Apple	13.	Uncle Sam
6.	Gentrification Riches	14.	Polish the Diamond
7.	Special Needs	15.	Leverage and Velocity
8.	Buy Acres & Sell Lots	16.	Money Before the Sale

- You can scale-up from one small apartment to more small apartments and/or one small apartment to mid-size and large apartments.

Bonus Resources Summary

FREE: *Become an Affiliate of My Products*
www.BMSABook.com/affiliate

Report: *20 Reasons You Should Use an LLC for Real Estate*
www.BMSABook.com/20llc

Webinar: *The Hidden Power of LLC's*
www.BMSABook.com/llc

Webinar: *Land Trusts Made Simple*
www.BMSABook.com/trusts

Webinar: *Real Estate Tax Strategies Your CPA Doesn't Know*
www.BMSABook.com/taxes

Webinar: *How to Wholesale Apartments*
www.BMSABook.com/flip

Webinar: *How to be an Apartment Turnaround Specialist*
www.BMSABook.com/turn

Interview: *$13,750 Made Flipping an Apartment with Snakes*
www.BMSABook.com/snakes

Interview: *Bad Management Makes for a Good Deal*
www.BMSABook.com/rehab

Interview: *Part-Time Flipper Makes $26,500 in 60 Days*
www.BMSABook.com/peas

Chapter 9

Four Components of Success in Real Estate

Whether you're just starting in small apartments or you're an industry expert, you're about to learn the exact secrets that will make you a *doer*, above the rest - the *dreamers*.

I've shown you up to this point how I and my students are quietly going out and buying or flipping apartment complexes for massive profits with absolutely none of our own money. And just like you, we started with an interest in single family but then immediately jumped to small apartments – for all of the reasons you've learned here in this book.

During my own journey to real estate success, I discovered that only the partial truth is told about real success in most real estate trainings. This may be blasphemy in revealing this but *success is not about just learning a skillset* to do apartment deals. Anyone can learn that from a book. *If knowledge was sufficient, librarians would be billionaires.*

Have you been to real estate investing trainings where they teach you 14 ways to do a nothing down deal or five ways to negotiate a contract? Well, I'm sure you probably have. That is important and necessary information but there's one thing they usually don't teach you at traditional real estate trainings.

And that is that *specialized knowledge alone is not sufficient for real estate success.* There's more to it than that.

What they don't teach and what cost me tens of thousands of dollars to learn and experience thru the school of hard knocks is that there are actually four components to real estate success. Specialized knowledge is just *one* of those four components. Let me now reveal the real estate success model, around which all of my teachings are based.

Bonus Resource
Webinar: *The Whole Truth About Real Estate Investing*
www.BMSABook.com/truth

Real Estate Success Model

The real estate success model, with the four components, is depicted in the triangle shown:

4 Components of
Real Estate Success™

The four components of success are:

- **Component #1**: Specialized Knowledge
- **Component #2**: Marketing
- **Component #3**: Systems
- **Component #4**: Mindset

Let's start with *specialized knowledge.*

Component #1: Specialized Knowledge

This is the specialized information that is unique to your field of endeavor. With apartments, it has to do with knowing how to find deals, fund deals, and farm deals, i.e. the exit strategies. And the more specialized your knowledge, the more money goes into your pocket – if you *act* upon it. This book is loaded with specialized knowledge – knowledge that took me and my mentors countless man-decades to try and perfect. You have the specialized knowledge for small apartments now.

Acquiring specialized knowledge is the easy part. Everyone does that. The shame of it is that too many people fall victim to the belief that to be a millionaire, I just need to buy the course. However, there is no magic pill to real estate success.

Do you have any real estate courses collecting dust on your book shelf? With awesome specialized knowledge? Come on. It's okay to admit it. It'll be our little secret. Well, let's examine that.

The secret to massive, repeatable and consistent success in your real estate business comes from simultaneously applying each of the remaining three components of real estate success with your specialized knowledge.

Component #2: Marketing

As noted business guru, Peter Drucker, points out… Business is just two things: marketing and innovation. If you are not marketing regularly and consistently; if your phone is not ringing regularly, you don't have a business, you have a *hobby*. Business is marketing. Period.

And as I've pointed out numerously in the strategies and case studies contained throughout this book, you are always marketing for two things: *deals and dollars*. Deals mean motivated sellers. Dollars mean the buyers and/or private investors.

And if you are a buy and hold apartment entrepreneur, there's a third thing you are always marketing for: *residents*. Yes, your property management company will do the work but you have to ensure that they are using massive marketing. I've shown how the value of your apartments is increased from forcing high occupancies and rents.

So the three things you are marketing for are:

1. Deals (always)
2. Dollars (always)
3. Residents (when you buy and hold)

Marketing should comprise two-thirds of your activities. That's right: two-thirds. The problem is that two-thirds of most entrepreneurs' time is spent on fire fighting, or everything except marketing. That's why you need the third component, *systems*.

Component #3: Systems

I presume that you chose real estate because you wanted more; a better lifestyle for yourself and/or your family. And real estate can absolutely provide that; a way to replace your J-O-B.

But don't fall into the trap of so many struggling real estate entrepreneurs. And that is, substituting one JOB working for someone else with another JOB where you are maybe working for a *lunatic* – yourself. You know, that boss who is always on your back 24/7, never happy and always has something else for you to urgently do. I'm smiling in writing this because I'm remembering my days starting out.

When you are working for someone else (and before you discover real estate), it's easy to take for granted the systems that are in place to support you in your specific role. For example, things such as bookkeeping, IT, promotion, contracting, legal, administration, call handling, office management, client care, etc.

But in your real estate business, you are the CEO. And as the new entrepreneur – the CEO -- of your business, it is your task to categorize and design the *systems* that free you up for marketing and a better lifestyle.

Your systems will be comprised of three leverage devices, or fulcrums. Recall Archimedes who said, *"Give me a big enough fulcrum and I'll move the earth."* The three fulcrums you will use in your business systems are:

- **Fulcrum #1**: Processes
- **Fulcrum #2**: Technology
- **Fulcrum #3**: People

Fulcrum #1: Processes

Processes are your standard operating procedures; they are *"how we do things around here."* It includes the checklists, the scripts, the forms, the templates, and the operating manual of how anyone can step in and replicate a particular process in a repeatable manner. Without processes, you are dependent on human memory and interpretation and that's a recipe for scattered results. Or you are dependent on your people to *"make it up."*

Let's look now at automation.

Fulcrum #2: Technology

Information technology and software has leveled the playing field for the small business owner. It perhaps started before you were born and you may take it for granted, but there was a time when the techniques and strategies revealed here could not have been implemented without large amounts of time, cash or capital. Today, anyone can do this business from anywhere, to any market in the country (or even worldwide). And do it on a large scale. Never before has it been easier for a part-timer to start in small apartments.

For example, you can access listing services for any market in the country from your phone and then make the call to a broker – while sitting at a cafe. Direct mail, which used to be reserved to the expensive direct mail houses, can now be inexpensively ordered on-line through a few clicks of the mouse.

You can automatically respond to buyer inquiries 24/7 while you are with your family (and automatically add every inquirer's contact information to your buyer's list). You can massively communicate with your entire buyer's list by simultaneously broadcasting text messages, voice messages and/or email. You can exchange offers and contracts and easily share them without the need for snail mail. I could go on and on.

As a prelude into the next fulcrum, *people*, the Internet has now made it possible to have people working for you inexpensively, part-time, and as needed – *anywhere* in the world.

Fulcrum #3: People

Just like real estate leverages other people's money for financial gain, a real estate *business* leverages other people's time and talent to fulfill the entrepreneur's vision – your vision for yourself and your family.

Even if you are starting as a solopreneur (like I did) and doing everything yourself initially, you must enter your new venture with the *intention and strategy to systematize those processes* which are non-critical for you to perform.

And with the advent of technology and ease of global communication, you can now hire *virtual* assistants (VA) – from anywhere on the planet. If you are not familiar with virtual assistants, they are people who work from their home and have multiple clients. They can be a full-time VA but only work for you part-time, billing you just for the time they work on your projects.

You might have one VA in the United States who takes inbound calls from direct mail and prequalifies sellers prior to you making an offer. That VA might also do the qualifying follow-up calls to your buyer leads. You might have another VA in the Philippines (who only charges $4 per hour) that performs back-office administrative tasks such as looking up lists of apartment owners, or pre-screening apartments from the listing services, prior to you calling a broker.

Yes, you may be doing most, if not all, of these activities yourself when you are starting out but you have to have a plan and understanding to shed those non-critical activities and roll-out your systems.

If we work together, I'll *give you my proven systems* which are continually updated and expanded. They are the same systems that each of the Case Studies in this book utilized. If we don't work together, then follow the recipe I'm providing here to develop your own systems.

There are lots of potential systems. So which ones should you start *first*? Since you are in the marketing business and two-thirds of your activities need to be devoted to marketing, you should begin with your *marketing systems.*

Your Key Marketing Systems

Systems range from operations to marketing but you begin with marketing systems since that's where you gain leverage and cash flow. There are four key marketing systems I want to point out:

- **System 1**: Deal Generator System
- **System 2**: Buyer-Investor Generator System
- **System 3**: Closing System
- **System 4**: Traffic Generator System

System 1: Deal Generator System

This is the system that markets for the *deals*. The *Deal Generator System* finds and qualifies apartment leads, makes offers and generates a contract. Its output is a signed contract.

System 2: Buyer-Investor Generator System

This is the system that markets for the *dollars*. The *Buyer-Investor Generator System* finds prospective buyers and investors for your deals, qualifies them, negotiates with them and obtains the written agreement. Its output is a signed agreement.

System 3: Closing System

This is the system that takes the deal from signed contract to closing, either on a buy-and-hold or a wholesale flip, including due diligence. Its output is a closed deal.

System 4: Traffic Generator System

This is the system that markets for the *residents* on the apartments you own. The *Traffic Generator System* finds prospective residents, qualifies them, negotiates with them and obtains the written lease agreement leading to move-in. Its output is a leased apartment unit.

Again, if we work together, I'll give you my systems for the above so you can get started right away. In some cases, I'll *do it for you*. If you are doing it yourself, follow this template. It works. Which system is your first priority? Deal flow. Your business *starts with deal flow*.

This leads to the fourth and most important component of success: *Mindset*.

Component #4: Mindset

Now, we get to the heart of the matter; the heart of success – the mindset and habits for taking action and overcoming the *limiting beliefs* and the *fears* that are holding us all back from our ultimate dreams. And that's why I place *Mindset* in the heart of the above triangle.

The Enemy is FEAR

Everyone has fear. I have it and you have it. It's the human condition. It might be fear of *embarrassment*, fear of *failure*, fear of making a *mistake*, even fear of *success*. Fear is nothing but limiting beliefs expressing themselves *subconsciously* through our internal little voice.

The sole difference between two entrepreneurs in the same market and with the same knowledge is how they *respond* to their inner fears – their mindset. One can be out doing the deals while the other is doing nothing, complaining that *"This stuff doesn't work"* or *"It doesn't work in this market, blah, blah."* That's mindset – the ability to take action despite the fear.

Let me now share how it all began for me in real estate and how *I know the meaning of fear,* and overcoming it.

Case Study – Trembling Knees Yield 23 Nothing-Down Deals

When I started out in real estate, I took a training course. It contained the specialized knowledge to do a first deal. And then I took several more and bought the home study courses. Yet a year later, I still had not done one thing to begin my marketing.

I had more than enough knowledge but I didn't act because of fear. My fear was the *fear of embarrassment.* The prospect of getting on the phone with a seller and them asking me a question I couldn't answer paralyzed me. (In fact, the fear of embarrassment is the root of practically all fears.) So the way my subconscious compensated was by telling me – *for one year* - that I just needed to learn more. If I got more training, I would know *everything* and no one could stump me. I approached real estate as I was preparing for a final exam.

Can anyone know all there is to know about real estate? No, of course not; it's absurd to think so. Yet, that's how my little voice was directing me.

Finally, after a year of courses and charges to my credit card, I decided enough was enough. So I prepared my first marketing campaign. As I mentioned earlier, my family was heading to Hawaii in three weeks and I decided to mail Houston real estate owners in Honolulu and invite them to meet me on July 16 if they were dissatisfied with their Houston real estate. I prepared a meager 50 letters.

I remember the day I stood in front of that mail box slot at the post office with trembling knees and those letters clinched in my hands over the slot. This was a moment of truth. To combat the fear, I said to myself, *"Other mere mortals have done this so you can do it. I just need to take this first step and act in faith that I'll figure out the next step."* And with that, I released the letters.

Now, if you are familiar with direct mail you know that a 1% response is considered a good response. So what is 1% of 50? How many people should I expect to call? That's right, *half a person.* I can tell you there are *hundreds* of people in Honolulu who own property in Houston so why did I only mail to 50? I now know why: my subconscious could do the math as well and my little voice was telling me, *"If you send 50 letters, you can say you did something but not have to actually speak to anyone."* It's called *self-sabotage* by not fully committing.

Back to my story. Instead of 1%, my response rate was 30%! Fifteen people called me. I scheduled 30 minute appointments back-to-back for eight hours for July 16 in Honolulu. I arranged for each of them to meet me in the lobby of the hotel. So now, I find myself on the morning of July 16, just prior to my meetings, confronting the fear again. I'm not meeting these people over the phone; I'm going to meet them *face-to-face.* The fear was running rampant. So I again said to myself, *"Other mere mortals have done this so you can do it. I just need to take this next step and act in faith that I'll figure out the next step."*

I met the first five people. They were all nice. They all had real estate problems, they all were appreciative of the fact that I was there. Not one asked me an embarrassing question. If they asked me something I couldn't answer, I just replied I'd have to get back with them. Each of the five did ask, *"Can you help me?"* I replied, *"I'm not sure yet. I have to go back and look at your situation but if I do buy your property, I'll be asking you to carry back the financing. How do you feel about that?"* To a person they said, *"That's fine. I just want out."*

Wow, that blew me away. And at that point, I had an immediate mindset shift. I had confronted my fear thru my first seller engagements and the world had not ended. Rather, I discovered that what I had been taught actually worked. So, between the fifth and sixth appointments, I said to myself, *"I'm going to do a deal right here today."* I met the remaining 10 appointments with continually growing confidence.

Would you like to know how many deals I did from those fifteen appointments that day? I did 23. I bought 23 properties from that group of 15 who responded to my first meager mailing of 50 letters. And from there, I never looked back.

I had confronted the fear by acting in faith and trusting myself to handle the next step. Now, let's go back to that moment where I stood over the mailbox slot with trembling knees. If I had not taken that next step there, I probably wouldn't be here – over a decade later – writing this book. I might still be working a job. I might have been laid-off in the Great Recession. Instead I'm here living my vision - all because of my mindset shift and confronting the fear, by taking the next step and acting in faith.

Your Greatest Asset is Your Mind

Think about it, a business is only as strong as the mindset of its CEO. And as the CEO of your real estate business, it is incumbent – correction, it is ESSENTIAL – that you *condition* your mindset for automatic success. Wealth and financial freedom comes from *habits* of success.

Want to be an apartment millionaire? Well, you need to first have the mindset of an apartment millionaire. Freedom and wealth originates from within. It is about reconditioning yourself into new daily and empowering habits. And it is easily done.

The most important part is realizing that the true source of all success starts on the inside. With that realization, you are now ready to personally establish new and empowering thought patterns.

The true beauty of it is that your life is a canvas and you are the artist. *The past does not matter.* You are in control of the most powerful tool on the earth – your own *mind*. Yet, it is your responsibility to follow the path and techniques *paved by others* in learning how to leverage your own power in creating abundance thru real estate.

First, the *bad news*...

We are typically not taught the mindset of an entrepreneur in school. We are taught the mindset of an employee. School was designed to make us good employees. That's not a value judgment on schools; it's just a fact.

Now, the *good news*...

The mindset of action, abundance and entrepreneurism can be *learned* – and quickly. It is really a matter of replacing your limiting beliefs with more empowering and *supportive beliefs* that support your vision; belief systems that silence the fears that are *subconsciously* prohibiting you from taking the action that leads to different and more powerful results. In Chapter 10, I'll teach you the *system* for doing it.

Not only have I experienced all this for myself but I've observed it for countless students who I've coached and mentored – including all of the ones referenced in this book. Hear for yourself from the students in these bonus interviews about the importance of mindset.

Bonus Resource
Interview: *$255,000 Equity Gain from Forced Appreciation*
www.BMSABook.com/forced

Bonus Resource
Interview: *The Secret to 100% Owner Financing*
www.BMSABook.com/ken

So, let me repeat what I said in Chapter 1…

You Need a Mentor

Everyone needs a mentor. The greatest athletes and business leaders still have coaches and mentors. If those at the apex need a mentor, you and I need mentors.

When I was starting out, I was fortunate to have multiple mentors. I had mentors that coached me on specialized knowledge, on marketing and on systems. And I had separate mentors that mentored me on mindset. But I had to seek them out – it literally took *years* of searching. And guidance by mentors has never ceased for me, they have just changed as I grew internally. To this day, I have mentors.

I am offering to mentor you, with you as my apprentice.

Bonus Resource
Complimentary Planning Session
www.BMSABook.com/plan

Through my own journey into real estate, I discovered that my gift - my talent - is to transform seemingly complex and unrelated concepts, techniques and processes into unique, *easy to understand systems* that accelerate the learning and mentoring process. And my additional gift is the ability to mentor, guide and inspire both new and experienced apartment entrepreneurs to *profound change - in compressed periods of time.*

I do it using the *Real Estate Success Model* I just revealed and the *Apprentice Model*, which has stood the test of time as the path to success. I am not referring to the Donald Trump Apprentice model in which you compete to the death to be the sole survivor.

True apprenticeship is about nurturing and supportive training that requires a wide range of skills and knowledge, as well as maturity and independence of judgment. It is guidance. It is support. It is encouragement.

With apartments, it includes having someone mentor you in order to:

- Establish your financial freedom plan
- Model your daily plan and *habits*
- Create your *deal flow*
- *Analyze* deals
- *Negotiate* deals
- Attract *buyers* and negotiate *flips*
- Attract and structure *private money* deals
- Stay *focused*
- Redirect you when you are discouraged
- Create new *belief systems*
- Recondition your *mindset* for success
- Establish your critical *systems*
- Show you how to be laser-focused with your *time*
- *Scorecard* your progress
- Work with you *in-the-field*
- Simultaneously cover all *four components* of real estate success

Every one of the case studies in this book is a testament to the power of the apprenticeship model. I know of their successes because I was there when they occurred. I mentored them. They received the specialized knowledge, the marketing, the systems and mindset for success in small apartments.

If you'd like to learn about my coaching and mentoring programs, see the *Resources Section* in the back of the book. There you can hear the success stories of just some of the apprentices who have preceded you.

Coming Up...

In the next chapter, I'll start my mentoring by teaching you how to recondition and program your mindset for greater success. I'll show you how to create the new habits that will drive you to any desired outcome you select for yourself. Do not skip the next chapter! Read it now.

Chapter Summary

- There are four components to success in real estate that few talk about:
  1. Specialized Knowledge
  2. Marketing
  3. Systems
  4. Mindset

- Specialized knowledge is an essential component of success but not the only one. If it was all that was needed, librarians would be billionaires.

- Business is marketing and innovation. You are in the marketing business and two-thirds of your activities need to be devoted to marketing.

- Again… You are always marketing for two things: *deals and dollars*. You market for a third thing when you own apartments: *residents*.

- A real business has *systems* which leverage you as the CEO.

- The three fulcrums for your systems are:
  1. Processes
  2. Technology
  3. People

- The first systems you should roll-out are your *marketing systems*.

- There are four marketing *sub-systems*:
  1. Deal Generator System
  2. Buyer-Investor Generator System
  3. Closing System
  4. Traffic Generator System

- Any business is only as strong as the *mindset* of its CEO (you). The enemy to your success in real estate is FEAR.

- Mindset means having the ability to take action despite any fears or obstacles. It is at least 70% of your success. Good news: It is learnable.

- If you want to be an apartment millionaire, you have to have the mindset of an apartment millionaire.

- You need proven systems and a mentor for all four components of success.
- I'm offering to mentor you.

Bonus Resources Summary

Webinar: *The Whole Truth About Real Estate Investing*
www.BMSABook.com/truth

Interview: $255,000 Equity Gain from Forced Appreciation
www.BMSABook.com/forced

Interview: *The Secret to 100% Owner Financing*
www.BMSABook.com/ken

Complimentary Planning Session
www.BMSABook.com/plan

Chapter 10

The Whole Truth About Real Estate Investing

In the previous chapter, I presented the *Real Estate Success Model* and the four components of success: 1) specialized knowledge, 2) marketing, 3) systems, and 4) the most important component: *mindset; more* specifically the *entrepreneurial mindset*. It's probably 70% of success in real estate. In this chapter, I'll reveal the *system* for *conditioning* your entrepreneurial mindset.

Playing BIG

If you really intend to play bigger, this chapter contains the most important information that I have to teach you. Do NOT skip this. You may be saying, *"I want to learn about small apartments. What does this have to do with apartments?"*

It has nothing to do with apartments from a *technical* standpoint, but it has EVERYTHING to do with apartments and real estate if you want to be successful. You can *desire* to play bigger but, unfortunately, desire is not enough.

To play BIG, you have to begin by setting BIG goals - goals that are *just beyond* what you currently believe possible and outside the proverbial *"comfort zone."* That is what I mean by mindset. Sadly, too many are people playing small. This "playing small" *mentality* comes from decades of conditioning by our schools and employers to think and act like good students and employees.

In school, we are conditioned to believe that storing knowledge is sufficient; and we are rewarded for *testing* well. In the workplace, we are further conditioned to believe that following the checklist step-by-step and not making a mistake is the path to success; follow the instructions and you receive a paycheck every two weeks.

Entrepreneurship requires a different mindset. Entrepreneurship is *messy*, it's *non-linear*, and mistakes are made; it's how you respond in an environment of uncertainty and obstacles that determines your success. Hence, your old conditioning from schools and employers has to be *replaced* with *new beliefs* – bigger beliefs of what's possible - and are *supportive* of your role as a successful apartment entrepreneur.

Bonus Resource
Webinar: *The Whole Truth About Real Estate Investing*
www.BMSABook.com/truth

I said you need BIG goals. That's true but that's not all you need for success.

Goal Setting vs. Goal Achievement

Here's the problem: *goal setting does not equal goal achievement.* They're two entirely different processes and strategies. They even originate from two different parts of your brain:

- Conscious Mind: *Goal Setting*
- Subconscious Mind: *Goal Achievement*

Goal setting occurs in the *conscious* part of your mind. You consciously think about what you desire and write down your goals. You *will* things to happen, as if willpower is all that's needed (*"This year, I'll force myself to lose that weight"*). Willpower is a powerful *short-term* mechanism for stretching yourself but willpower, alone, will *not* enable you to achieve any results which require a *sustained* effort.

Have you ever been on a diet plan, or known someone who was on a diet plan, and realized short-term results but then later ballooned back to their original weight. That's an example of the mismatch between conscious willpower and a person's subconscious identity. Their inner world was not in alignment with their desired outer world results (being thinner). The same occurs with financial change in your life.

Goal achievement, and sustained change, originates from your *subconscious* mind – the super computer. Willpower can never outdo your subconscious belief systems and habits because your subconscious habits are *10,000 times more powerful* than your conscious willpower. Sustained change in your life comes from creating new *habits* – behaviors which occur *automatically* and which you are largely unaware.

New Money Comes from New Habits

These habits determine the extent of the financial abundance that you manifest. Left unchanged, your financial trajectory will change only +/- 10% - for life - until you develop new habits. Real change in your financial situation comes from addressing your habits and the underlying belief systems of what's possible for you.

The basis of all systems for success and achievement stems from the axiom, *"We become what we mostly think about."* Thoughts are like seeds in the brain. Nurture and feed them daily and they will sprout. Neglect them and they die. Each of us is having the same 6,000 thoughts or so every day – and as a result, those seeds are continually sprouting in our life. Hence, it is important to choose your thoughts wisely.

However, you can't consciously control your thoughts. Try it. Try thinking the same thought for 10 minutes. It's impossible.

Hence, you can't force sustained change thru willpower. *Positive thinking* is not enough. So how do you choose and control your thoughts?

Change first begins with awareness so my first step is to make you aware of how you manifest results in your life; it's called the *Law of Manifestation*. Once you understand this cycle, you'll understand why you do what you do. Following that, I'll reveal the *system* for making your brain work for you.

Law of Manifestation

The Law of Manifestation shows the cycle playing out in your life.

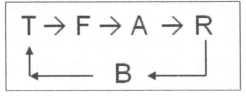

Law of Manifestation

Your thoughts (T) lead to your feelings (F), and your feelings lead to your actions (A). Your actions yield your results (R), and those results are what condition, or strengthen, your beliefs (B). Your beliefs trigger your thoughts, and the cycle continues.

This reveals why you can't consciously control your thoughts for any appreciable period of time. Your conscious thoughts are continually being interrupted by external stimuli (the TV, a billboard, a conversation, an email) which are *filtered* through your belief systems and trigger new thoughts. We each respond differently to external stimuli because my filters are different than yours – due to our different belief systems.

So if sustained change does not come from consciously changing your thoughts, where does it occur?

Filing Cabinet

All sustained change originates from your belief systems – which are in your subconscious. Think of your belief systems as a filing cabinet which stores all your life experiences and the corresponding results. Each experience has a *file*. The more times the experience is repeated (conditioned), the thicker the file becomes. And if an experience is accompanied by heavy emotion, the file is given a red flag as important. These files are largely created and established prior to the *age of six* and are the basis of why you *act* the way you do. And *that's the issue*. Let me share a hypothetical story to explain.

Story

I'm three years old and I'm playing alone on the kitchen floor. Being a toddler, I'm naturally curious. Everything is an adventure. I look up from the kitchen floor to the countertop and wonder how great the view would be from there. I'm off to a new adventure – to climb up to the countertop. I drag my high stool close to the counter and begin climbing. When I reach the top, I straddle the chasm between the chair and countertop with one leg on the chair and one leg on the countertop. I laughingly and confidently prepare to "take the leap." Just then, my father comes around the corner and sees me teetering over the chasm. His protective instincts automatically take over and he jerks me from my leap of faith, sets me down, swats my behind, and tells me, *"Don't ever let me see you do that again."*

It's an emotional point for both me and him. So how does that experience get filed away in my internal cabinet of beliefs? My brain records: stretching myself and reaching out leads to *pain*. And because that was an emotional experience, it gets a red tag. Repeat similar types of experiences over many years and I'm left with a thick file which equates *pain* with stretching myself and reaching out.

Now, roll the calendar forward 35 years. I'm 38 years old and *consciously* deciding to shift from employment to entrepreneurship - an environment of *stretching and reaching out*. The subconscious goes to the file cabinet, checks the file with the red tag and whispers thru my little voice, *"Entrepreneurship requires you to reach out and stretch beyond your comfort zone. You know from experience that leads to pain. Don't do it."* And that's the *thought (T)* I'm sent which leaves me *feeling (F)* that maybe it's not really for me so I take no *action (A)*. And I will subconsciously seek out other examples (*results*) *(R)* to prove that *belief (B)* right.

You see, your subconscious brain's number one job is to protect you from pain. But's it relying on data and interpretations that are incorrect - files that are decades old and were wrongly filed to begin with. You have to update the files and stuff them with new supportive data - new *subconscious* beliefs, which *support* the results you *consciously* desire. How do you choose your beliefs?

Be → Do → Have

In school, we were taught this model for success:

$$Do → Have → Be$$

They taught us: work hard (Do) and you'll be able to possess more (Have) and then you'll (Be) successful. To be a millionaire, they'd have us believe that working harder is the sure-fire path for financial success. Yet, the actions of becoming a millionaire are *different* than the actions of just being financially comfortable.

For example, we were taught the 40 Year Plan to financial freedom which I discussed in Chapter 4, thinking that working hard (Do) as an employee for 40 years would allow me to (Be) able to retire. How is that working for you?

That model does not work. It's backwards. The correct model is:

$$Be → Do → Have$$

The path to manifesting financial abundance or any new result in your life, starts from *first* consciously choosing the results you desire and then second, consciously choosing the *beliefs that support* those results.

We are human *"beings."* We are not human *"doings."* Prior to possessing $1 million (Have), you must first identify yourself as a millionaire (Be). Your inner world (your beliefs and identify) must first be congruent with your outer world (your results) before your subconscious will allow you to continually have the thoughts, feelings and actions necessary to manifest that result.

Case Study – "I Didn't Work Hard Enough"

I had a new student once who had a $1.5 million apartment under contract that she wanted to wholesale. It was a good deal. She asked me, *"How much should I charge for my wholesale fee?"* Seeing a teaching opportunity, I asked, *"How much do you think you should charge?"* She replied, *"Do you think $5,000 would be too much?"*

I exclaimed, *"$5,000?! Why do you think $5,000 is the right amount?"* Her answer bears out what I am teaching you. She said, *"Well, I didn't think that I had worked hard enough to make more than $5,000."*

At her core, she believed that she had to work hard to make a lot of money (the incorrect Do Have Be model). She also associated $5,000 as a lot of money, as part of her identify. Her beliefs were *non-supportive* of her desired result of financial abundance.

Supportive Beliefs vs. Non-Supportive Beliefs

Beliefs are neither right or wrong, nor are they true or false. They are either *supportive* or *non-supportive* of the results you consciously desire.

Here are some common non-supportive belief systems:

- "I have to work harder to have more"
- "Money is the root of all evil"
- "I am not good / smart enough."

Can you see how having one or more of these beliefs systems will dictate your actions (or inaction) in manifesting abundance?

Here's another example I'm sure you can relate with: lottery winners. We hear the stories of big multi-million dollar lottery winners who have financial abundance thrust upon them. Their "results" change overnight. And what results do they have one year later? That's right, they return back to where they started (or worse). They *consciously* desire wealth but their inner world identity, or *subconscious* belief system, is not in alignment with their new outer world riches. And because their inner world has to be congruent with their outer world, they *subconsciously* shed their new abundance until their outer world matches their inner world.

This is a key reason why I recommend people start with *small* apartments. Besides confidence building, it allows you time to condition your inner world for the greater abundance afforded thru mid-size and large apartments.

Why Your First Deal is Critical

As I discussed above, you begin the process of change by first choosing new belief systems that are supportive of the results you want. Then you recondition those beliefs into your subconscious mind. In a moment, I'll show you the process.

But here's how to speed up the entire process. Go back and look at the *Law of Manifestation*. It shows how your results (R) condition your belief system (B) – the source of all success. The way to fast-track the cycle is to quickly achieve a new result, because then your belief system is supercharged. What we call confidence is actually a belief that something is possible.

That's why I am so emphatic about getting you into your first deal. Within a nanosecond of your first closing (R), your brain asks, *"How can I do more deals just like this."* That's a new belief (B) expressing itself. Your belief system goes on steroids with that first deal.

You Need a Mentor

It's because of this *supercharger effect* on your beliefs from closing your first deal that I say you need a mentor. A mentor does a number of things.

First, he or she catalyzes the process of getting you to your critical first deal. The sooner you get a new *result (R)*, the faster your *beliefs (B)* change; instantly changing your *thoughts (T)* and *feelings (F)* of what's possible, resulting in even more *actions (A)* congruent with those results. A mentor acts like a catalyst on this cycle.

Second, a mentor also reconditions your belief systems in the process of getting you to your first deal by silencing the doubtful self-talk that *naturally* arises when you are stretching yourself into something new. The mentor provides confidence (*belief* that you can do it). He or she "has your back."

Third, a mentor can see your limiting beliefs and make you aware of them so that you understand why you are scared of calling that first broker or making that first offer. He can show you "how it's done" when you are starting out.

Can you do it on your own? Yes, of course - especially when you work on your mindset in parallel with entering the business. That's why I make *mindset conditioning lessons* a core of all of my training programs.

Evaluating Your Belief Systems

Would you like to *know* what your embedded belief systems are? You can know your belief systems right *now* by simply examining the results in your life at this moment. Your results today are a reflection of your inner beliefs. Everything you manifested to date arose from your beliefs of what's possible. And since I presume that you are reading this book to change your financial results, you need to replace your *current* beliefs with *new ones* which are more *supportive* of your desired results.

Let me now show you the *system* for reconditioning your mindset - your *subconscious* inner beliefs - to be congruent with the results you *consciously* desire.

The System for Reconditioning Your Mindset

The best news is that you can *recondition* your mindset and develop the belief systems which are congruent with your desired results. All of this leads to new actions (*habits*) of success. There is a five-step *system* in which you can take control of your brain and put it to work for you. It is:

- **Step 1**: Vision and "Reason Why"
- **Step 2**: Vision Board
- **Step 3**: Story Board
- **Step 4**: Plan
- **Step 5**: Action

I developed this system from mentors who I paid to work with me on my inner game when I started out in real estate. I paid substantially for what I am *gifting* to you here.

Step 1: Vision and "Reason Why"

It all begins with your *Vision* and your *"Reason Why."* Now, let me warn you that most people want to skip this step. Do NOT skip this. Without it, you'll drift back to where you began.

No one enters the apartment arena because they like working with buildings or contracts. They enter it because they seek a different result. You have to get very specific on the *"Reason Why"* you are pursing apartments. And it's not money. Money is just a tool to a desired result.

A strong "Reason Why" is more powerful than the "how" you'll do it. In fact, when your "why" is strong enough, you will find the "how."

Case Study – My Reason Why

When I started looking for an additional income stream years ago, my "Reason Why" was my young daughter. I wanted to be able to provide her the greatest education possible. When the time came for her to enter college, I wanted to be able to fund that education – no matter the university or cost. I imagined the future day when she might say to me, "*Dad, this is the one I want.*" And I would be able to reply, "*Sweetheart, this is the one you get.*"

The prospect of having to deny her that opportunity was so painful that I was willing to do whatever it took to avoid that pain. That was tremendous leverage on me to keep going whenever I hit real estate challenges and my little voice said, "*This won't work*" or "*Give up.*"

Roll the calendar ahead years later to 2008 and I'm standing on the campus of Wake Forest University with my daughter and wife. It's selection day for high school seniors. (If you don't know Wake Forest University, it's a fabulous private university in North Carolina; the tuition is $60,000 per year). Standing on the quad in front of the chapel at 5:00 in the afternoon, my daughter turned to me and said, "*Dad, this is the one I want.*" And I happily replied, "*Sweetheart, this is the one you get.*"

That event had been created years before when I established my "*Reason Why*" and consciously decided to condition my mindset, so that I could take the actions necessary in apartments to manifest that result. I recognized what had just played out and to commemorate it, I asked a stranger to take a picture of us at that moment. That picture is displayed proudly today.

I want you to come to grips with your "Reason Why." Why are you reading this book and why have you read it this far?

Hot Coals

In establishing your "Reason Why," here's what I've observed. We may not cross the street to help ourselves but we will walk across *hot coals* to help someone or something we care about. So, to have the greatest leverage over your self-talk, establish your "Reason Why" in terms of your children, your spouse, your parents, your favorite cause, your church or temple.

Don't do it because you only want something for yourself. That's fine but *also* do it for someone else who you would never disappoint. That pain of prospectively letting them down is great leverage over your little voice.

Writing Your Vision

After you've established your "Reason Why," here's the next step. Find a quiet place with pen and paper and start *writing* down your vision of that future state: *where do you want to be, who do you want to be with, what are you doing, what does it sound like, what does it feel like, taste like?*

You have to imagine that future state in your mind. As Einstein said, "*Imagination is more powerful than knowledge.*"

Do you want to be on a family vacation in Hawaii in three years? Then I want you to write down and imagine *seeing* the deep, dark blue of the Pacific. Imagine *smelling* the sea air. Imagine *hearing* the waves lapping up on the beach. Imagine the sound of doves cooing in the trees. Imagine *feeling* the cool sea breeze caressing your bare skin.

Involve all of your senses. The more senses you involve, the more *vividly* it is impressed upon your subconscious. You have to be vivid in your imagination of what you want to have. Remember, the brain *craves* specificity.

Now ask yourself: "*Why is this vision important?*"

You might write, "*Because of quality time with my family. Because I am creating memories for my kids.*"

Now repeat and ask yourself again: "*Why is that important?*"

Keep traveling down deeper, layer by layer, asking why that is important. When you reach a point that a tear starts to well up in your eye - that's where you want to be. You've hit gold – an emotional connection. Remember, an emotional connection to an experience puts a red flag on the internal file. Emotion is a powerful lever.

Here's the secret: *your subconscious cannot tell the difference between what is real and what is not real*. When your subconscious mind *believes* it is real for you – when that future state becomes part of your *identity* – it will trigger the *thoughts* which lead to the *feelings* which support the consistent, daily *actions* to make your outer world *results* match your inner world *beliefs*. It is the cycle of the Law of Manifestation.

Once you have that future state vividly written down, let's now capture it to a tool you will use for your daily conditioning, your *Vision Board*.

Step 2: Vision Board

The subconscious mind is very *visual*. That's why athletes visualize the shot before they take it. They create it in their inner mind to *believe* it so their actions create an external result that matches their internal visualization.

You are going to capture your written vision to your own Vision Board – a poster board, or pieces of paper, with photos of your future state. If it's that vacation in Hawaii, go online and get pictures of Hawaii or cut them out of a magazine and put them on a poster board. If it's your family in Hawaii, put pictures of your family on the board.

You will review that Vision Board *daily* to impress upon your subconscious beliefs the future state you designed. This daily exercise does two things. First, it enables you to quickly remind yourself of your "Reason Why." Second, because your subconscious cannot tell the difference between what is real and what is not real, that *future* state becomes part of your identity *today* – leading to actions *today* to manifest that future result.

197

Review your Vision Board daily. I keep one at the house and one at the office. If we ever meet at one of my trainings, I'll show you mine. Here's a story of how to make the most powerful Vision Board.

Case Study – Student Puts Himself in a Porsche

I once had a student who wanted to have a Porsche 911 car – his toy. So he had a couple of choices in creating his Vision Board. One, he could get a picture of a Porsche 911 online, print it out, and put it on the Vision Board. That's good but what's even better than that?

He went down to the Porsche dealer, sat in a Porsche 911, and had someone take a picture of him sitting inside that car. He put *that* on his Vision Board. Why is that more powerful? Because it's a representation of *him* in his future vision. That makes it even more real to the subconscious.

Safety Tip

I need to give you an important *safety tip*. The subconscious does not recognize a negative, such as "not" or "no." So if your vision is to pay off all your debts, do not put the words, *"No Debt"* on your Vision Board. Your subconscious only sees the word, *"Debt"* and that is what it focuses on. And since what you focus on *expands*, you will manifest more debt in your life. Instead, imagine *checks* coming in. Write some checks and take a picture of them spread across your kitchen table and affix *that* to your Vision Board.

Your Vision Board is the tool with which to create and impress daily images of your future state. Here's another story of how to create one.

Case Study – Student Enlists Family For Shared Vision

I had another student one time that included his family in the process of establishing a shared vision and a *family* Vision Board. He explained to his kids, *"Dad is going to start something new and I want your support."* By involving his spouse and young children, he not only enlisted their support but he created a strong "Reason Why" in specifically knowing how his real estate business would bring joy to his kids – that was powerful leverage over his little voice.

Once you have your Vision Board, you next design how you are going to reach that vision. This next step is really fun and provides a great sense of control over your life. It's your *Story Board*.

Step #3: Story Board

When you follow Step #2, you'll have a Vision Board which vividly depicts the future *result* you desire. But the brain then asks, *"How do we get there from here?"* It might appear impossible to achieve. Well, have you ever heard the saying, *"How do you eat an elephant? One bite at a time."* That's how you are going to do it. You are going to "chunk down" the process of going from today to your future state in bite-size pieces so it becomes plausible in your mind's eye.

To do it, you are going to create a *Story Board*. This is how directors and producers create movies - by creating and positioning every scene of the movie far before any actors are placed on the set. In the old days, the director would have every scene, every shot, sketched out on a piece of paper. The paper scenes were then pinned – in order – along the walls of large rooms, telling the entire movie's story. If a scene or shot didn't fit, it was moved around, or eliminated, or reimagined. The director saw it all in his mind's eye before the first camera ever arrived.

And just as a producer and director can storyboard a movie, you can storyboard your life. But you don't require a large room.

Take several sheets of paper or a poster board or a whiteboard. Orient the paper in landscape mode. The bottom of your paper is a timeline. The left-hand side is your current life; the right-hand side is the future. That is the time period of your vision. You are now going to break-down the journey from *here to there* in a series of logical milestones, recorded on small post-it notes.

The Journey

You start at the end and work backwards. Let's use the example goal of a family vacation in Hawaii. Take a post-it note and write, "Vacation in Hawaii." Take that post-it and stick it on the far right-hand side of your Story Board. That's the future vision.

Now start working backward. You ask yourself, *"What milestone must immediately precede that milestone?"* Maybe it's "Purchase Airline Tickets." You write that on a post-it note and place it just to the *left* of the previous post-it note. You then repeat the process, asking: *"What milestone must immediately precede this milestone?"* Maybe it's "Flip my Second Apartment." You write that on a post-it note and place it on your Story Board to the left of the previous milestone. And because your mind is coming up with the answers, there can be no incorrect answers here. This process is for the benefit of your mind's eye *seeing* how to get from here to there so your own mind will dictate what it considers the logical sequence.

You continue this process of working backwards, milestone-by-milestone – right to left, while asking, *"What milestone must immediately precede this milestone?"* As you get closer to the present, the milestones will probably become more granular. You'll have milestones like, "Make my First Offer," "Speak to My First Broker," "Analyze My First Deal." When you're done, you'll have a Story Board with a series of milestones captured on post-it notes – spanning your timeline.

You can then look at your journey in its entirety and *see* if it makes sense. If it doesn't feel right, you can adjust, eliminate or add milestones as your mind dictates. Remember, the whole purpose is to convince your brain and it'll tell you what seems logical – based on your beliefs at that point in time. You can see how you can logically progress from *here to there*. It becomes real and possible.

Now, let me share an important point. Do NOT affix dates to these milestones. Don't create a Gantt Chart like they use in project management. This is simply a road map with milestones that you use in getting started on your journey. Your subconscious can now assist you in seeking out the resources you'll need along the path.

Have you experienced the phenomenon of buying a new car, for example, a red Toyota, and you then start noticing all of the red Toyotas on the road. It's due to a region of your brain called the *reticular activating system* (RAS). The RAS is like a human search engine which finds anything related to what you "mostly think about." Did those red Toyotas magically just show up after your purchase? No, they were always there but you did not notice them because they were not part of your *focus*.

You are going to leverage your reticular activating system by making it work for you as you move from milestone to milestone along your Story Board. When you focus on a milestone, resources, events and people "magically" appear to assist you. In fact, they were always there but you were not focused on it.

Case Study – It's All Out There For You

When I created my Story Board for my training business, it included a milestone, "Speak on a National Stage." That seemed like a logical milestone. I reviewed that Story Board regularly. Not long after I started speaking and training, I received a call from a lady. She introduced herself and said, "*I am hosting a national real estate conference. I met one of your students and he tells me that you speak on apartments. Would you be interested in speaking at my conference?"* I immediately answered, *"Yes."* She said, *"I didn't give you the dates yet."* In my mind, it didn't matter because I recognized that I had arrived at that milestone. I knew I was at the right place. I hadn't been actively seeking a national speaking gig; it came to me – actually faster than I had expected. I got the dates from her and politely confirmed that I was available.

I then asked her, *"Out of curiosity, who else will be speaking?"* She rattled off some names which I recognized but then she came to one which left me speechless. She said, *"John Childers will also be there."* You see, John Childers was my first real estate trainer and mentor. He's the one who first pointed me in the direction of apartments. And he's also the one who first told me that I should offer training as an extension of my real estate business. I had come full circle. My Story Board had allowed me to know - with confidence - that I had arrived.

I should let you know that you are allowing me to further live out my Story Board. Another milestone on that original Story Board was "Write a Book." It's taken me longer than expected but now I am there.

Will your Story Board change along the journey? Yes, of course. As you achieve a milestone, especially the "first" of anything, such as your first *broker call*, your first *offer*, your first *closing*, that new *result* (R) will recondition your beliefs (B) and you'll think (T) that your Story Board is now too limiting. Your initial goals will probably appear too small. You'll adjust your Story Board to play bigger.

Getting started in apartments is a process of managing the "firsts" - the same firsts I mentioned above: your first broker call, first offer, first closing, etc. Those "firsts" are the hardest simply because they are new to you. A role of your mentor is to get you quickly thru each of the "firsts" so that your beliefs are rapidly reconditioned.

So now that you can *see* the journey, how do you further break it down into an action plan?

Plan

You have a Story Board. Now how do you determine your next step? You have to develop your plan. Here's the secret: *Focus on the next step that's immediately in front of you.* Too often I observe that people fall into overwhelm because they are worrying about step #43 while they have not yet completed or even started Step #1. That overwhelm, which comes from looking too far down the road, leads to confusion. And a confused mind always says, "No." Here's how you avoid overwhelm and develop your action plan of next steps, using your Story Board.

Begin by looking at the first two milestones on your Story Board. Then write down, for each of those first two milestones, the three actions you must take to move toward the completion of each. Focus on only those immediate two milestones and their actions.

For example, if Milestone 1 is "Analyze My First Deal," your actions could be: 1) Find a deal on Loopnet and 2) Run the numbers. It's that simple. If the next milestone is, "Speak to My First Broker," your actions could be: 1) Open an account on Loopnet, 2) Identify three brokers, and 3) Call a broker using my script.

As you complete an action, move on to the next one. As you complete a milestone, look to the next one and develop an action plan for it. Just work your way down the Story Board. Don't worry about Milestone 18 far down the road; it will take care of itself soon enough. Focus on what is immediately in front of you. Once you focus on what's in front of you, your reticular activating system will start bringing the resources and people and events into your life necessary to achieve the milestone.

I'm now going to share the time management system I used to escape from a demanding twenty year job, where there was "*no spare time.*"

Step #5: Performance Dashboard

Too often, I hear people say, *"I'd love to get started in apartments but I don't have the time."* Baloney. They have the time; they just don't have the right priorities and/or the right systems. When I started with apartments, I had a full-time and demanding job where I worked 60 hours per week. If I failed to meet my quarterly numbers, I was fired. Yet, I was able to escape within three short years using the time management system I developed then and I'm presenting now. It's called your *Performance Dashboard*. If I could do it, you can. And I did without the benefit of the insights you now have. I just "jumped in."

The Performance Dashboard is what keeps you focused on your critical weekly activities of what I call the *three M's*. Those critical activities are:

- Marketing
- Making offers
- Mindset conditioning

It's a simple paper-based system that manages and scorecards your *activities*. You create a grid on a sheet of paper with columns and rows. At the top, there are six columns for each day (*Monday thru Saturday*), another column for your goals for the week (*Goal*) and a "check-off" column (*X*).

In the rows along the left-hand side, you label your regular weekly activities. They include your marketing activities: *Direct Mail, New Broker Calls, Follow-up Broker Calls,* and *Deals Analyzed.* There is also a row for the activity, *Offers Made.* Finally, you write labels for the mindset conditioning activities in the remaining rows: *Vision Board, Story Board,* and *Plan.*

I have other activities but these will get you started and on the fastest path to cash. Now, the way you use your Performance Dashboard is that each Monday, you print a new scorecard. You assign weekly goals for each activity and record them in the *Goal* column. I'm going to save you the trouble of making one and give you your own Performance Dashboard.

Bonus Resource
Tool: *Performance Dashboard*
www.BMSABook.com/dashboard

Marketing

For example, let's say your goal is to send out 100 postcards this week. For the activity labeled *Direct Mail*, you write "100" in the column under the label *Goal*. If you send out 50 postcards on Monday, you write "50" under Monday for that activity. If you send another 50 on Tuesday, you write "50" under Tuesday. You've met your goal so under the "check-off" column labeled *X*, you check off that goal.

You're done with that activity for the week and it's important you stop working on it. You need a *balanced approach* across ALL activities. You want to meet *all* of your goals each week. Instead, if you decide to "stretch" and go beyond your goal of 100 because you're a super achiever, just realize that you are probably sacrificing some of your other goals. *A decision to do one thing is a decision to not do something else.*

You use this scorecard throughout your week to ensure that you have a balanced approach across ALL activities. When I adopted this, I found that Friday afternoon became my most productive time because I would pull out my Performance Dashboard and focus on completing those incomplete activities. This simple system created an inflection point in my real estate business and catalyzed my escape from corporate America.

Making Offers

Now, the most important activity on the Performance Dashboard is *Offers Made*. People sometimes ask, *"How long will it take me to complete my first deal?"* It's a logical question and unfortunately, I have no way of answering that. But I can say this with 100%

certainty, "*If you make no offers, you will make no money.*" You should establish your goal as a minimum of *one offer per week*. You do just one offer per week and that's fifty offers in a year. Something will close with fifty offers.

Mindset Conditioning

For the mindset conditioning activities, I recommend you set a goal of quickly reviewing your Vision Board, Story Board and Plan at least once daily.

All of these activities I've described are what you focus on weekly – they are your leverage points. Everything else is a distraction. For example, choosing the color of your business cards is not on the list. You do that after you've completed the other activities for the week. Just realize that your little voice will try to make you believe that the color of your business cards is important but it has nothing to do with you making money. It's just a trap your subconscious uses to keep you in your comfort zone.

Now, there's one piece of technology that I want you to add to your Performance Dashboard, a *productivity timer*.

Productivity Timer

Another logical question is, "*How much time do I need to get started?*" You need a minimum of sixty *productive* minutes per day. The keyword is "productive" and this is how anyone can get started. Studies have been done which show that CEO's of Fortune 500 corporations only have sixty productive minutes per day. The rest of the time is devoted to activities that are not directly attributable to growing the business. If Fortune 500 CEO's can run billion dollar companies on sixty productive minutes per day, you can start your small apartment business doing the same.

Get your Performance Dashboard and a sixty-minute egg timer; you can use the timer on your phone. Set it to sixty minutes and start working on the activities on your Performance Dashboard.

But there are some rules that you must follow. During those sixty minutes, you cannot reorganize your desk, check your Facebook, check your email from Mom, go to the bathroom, make a sandwich, or the other hundred traps that your subconscious will use to draw you back into your comfort zone.

You may be laughing but it's harder than it sounds – especially when you are just starting. After a few days, it'll start becoming more of a routine – a habit - and your little voice will start to silence.

If you take sixty productive minutes per day and focus on those activities on your Performance Dashboard, you'll start putting things out into the universe, such as broker calls, or direct mail, or offers, and the universe will respond to you. Now you are "in the game." You start to realize that this does work and it works for *you*.

That's the process. I've shown it all to you. I hope to someday meet you or maybe even work with you. Either way, I wish you the greatest of success in small apartments. You have what it takes right now. It's time for you to get started.

Bonus Resource
Complimentary Planning Session
www.BMSABook.com/plan

Bonus Resource
Interview: *Circle of Champions Roundtable Interview*
www.BMSABook.com/roundtable

Coming Up...

The next chapter sums it all up, "Why Small Apartments?"

Chapter Summary

- Seventy percent of success is mindset; you can condition your mindset with supportive beliefs for playing big.

- Goal Setting does NOT equal Goal Achievement; one is a *conscious* act, the other is a *subconscious* act.
- The Law of Manifestation explains how your subconscious beliefs produce your results; and how you can control your brain and recondition your beliefs to *Play BIG*.
- Playing BIG means adopting new belief systems and habits.
- New money comes from new habits.
- There is a Five-Step Process for reconditioning your belief systems and establishing new habits:
    - **Step #1**: Vision and "Reason Why"
    - **Step #2**: Vision Board
    - **Step #3**: Story Board
    - **Step #4**: Plan
    - **Step #5**: Performance Dashboard
- Financial change begins with a compelling Vision and your "Reason Why" – all captured in images on a Vision Board.
- You can *storyboard* your life so that your minds-eye can see that it's possible.
- You create and update your Action Plan based on the next two milestones on your Story Board.
- You scorecard yourself weekly with your Performance Dashboard.
- You can start your small apartment business with 60 *productive* minutes per day.
- You have what it takes right NOW.

Bonus Resources Summary

Complimentary Planning Session
www.BMSABook.com/plan

Interview: *Circle of Champions Roundtable Interview*
www.BMSABook.com/roundtable

Tool: *Performance Dashboard*
www.BMSABook.com/dashboard

Webinar: *The Whole Truth About Real Estate Investing*
www.BMSABook.com/truth

Chapter 11

Recap: Why Small Apartments?

I started the book with "Why Small Apartments" so if you like Cliff Notes, here's a quick summary of the Top 15 advantages:

Rental Demand is Up – Apartments are always strong because everyone needs a place to live. As a result of the Great Recession, less people can qualify to own a home. This, combined with demographic shifts of the young generation who rent, has led to *record* demand for rental apartments. You benefit from this demand whether wholesaling, buying to hold, or rehabbing.

Lots of Small Apartments for Deal Flow – You are in the marketing business, marketing for *deals and dollars*. There are lots of small apartments from which to prospect for deal flow.

Little Competition – Few people enter multifamily due to three limiting beliefs: 1) the belief they need to graduate from single family to multifamily, 2) the belief they need big bucks and credit to do these bigger deals, and 3) the belief they need to deal with tenants and toilets. All are false.

Hedge Funds Don't Pursue Small and Mid-Size Apartments – Hedge funds must move large sums of cash, millions of dollars, hence they traditionally focus on *large* apartments, and they recently shifted to also buying up large house portfolios from banks. In single family, this has eroded both deal flow and profits for the single family entrepreneur. The small and mid-size apartment market is untouched by hedge funds and *wide-open* to you, the apartment entrepreneur.

Can Quick-Flip Apartments Just Like Houses – You can wholesale small apartments just like houses. Small apartments close fast, enabling you to quickly close that critical *first deal.*

Lots of Buyers for Small Apartment Flips – When it comes to wholesaling, there are lots of buyers for your small apartments and they are easily distinguishable and accessible. The largest buying group of small apartment is *burned-out single family landlords* who want to get out of the property management business.

Big Wholesale Fees – With bigger ticket items comes larger profits. Expect five-figure checks (or higher) when you are flipping your small apartment contracts.

Little Cash to Raise When You Buy – As compared to mid-size and large apartments, the purchase price of small apartments is low. They require a smaller amount of cash to buy (if any). The best private investing source for small apartments is holders of *self-directed IRA's.* Find just one self-directed IRA holder with $50,000 to a few hundred thousand dollars and you have your bank.

Able to Hire Management Companies – Small apartments generate more revenue than houses and hence you are able to find and pay good apartment management companies from the revenue. You leverage the management company's *economies of scale* in keeping your expenses low while they do everything on your property. You are not a property manager, you are an *asset manager.* You manage the managers.

Combine Small Apartments with Your House Business – If you are making money with houses now, you can and should add small apartments as another profit center. Many of the same people who buy your wholesale houses will buy small apartments. Leverage your buyer's list.

Can Scale-up to Larger Deals – Everything you learn in small apartments is *extensible* to mid-size and large apartments. It's just extra zeros and you enjoy even greater *economies of scale*. Do your first deal on a *small* apartment to gain confidence, and then scale-up to more small apartments and/or mid-size and large apartments.

Make Offers Sight Unseen from Your Kitchen Table – The valuation of commercial apartments is based on the *numbers* – the income. You don't need to see the property; you just need to see the financials: the P&L and Rent Roll. You can evaluate deals and make offers on your own time from anywhere, to anywhere.

Perfect for Part-Time – You don't need to see the properties to evaluate them or to make offers. You just need to see the financials which you then evaluate on your own time. You create deal flow thru brokers and direct mail which you can coordinate from anywhere and anytime. This is not *driving for dollars*.

No Dodd-Frank Restrictions – The Dodd-Frank Law placed restrictions on owner financing of *owner-occupied* property like houses. Owner-financing is a great strategy for buying, selling, and flipping properties. These restrictions do not apply to apartments where they are not *owner-occupied*.

No Prior Experience Needed – You are qualified right now to start with small apartments. You do not need to graduate from single family to multifamily. You can start with multifamily just as I did as well as all the students cited in the Case Studies in the book.

Coming Up...

The next and final chapter addresses the most frequently asked questions about small apartments. Following that, you receive a summary of all of the Bonus Resources in the book. Take advantage of them.

Chapter 12

Frequently Asked Questions

I believe I've heard them all but here are short answers to the most frequently asked questions on getting started in small apartments. Full answers, explanations and Case Studies are provided throughout the book:

Q: I don't have a lot money or good credit. Can I really do apartments?

Yes, you just act as the entrepreneur, not the investor. As the entrepreneur, you are always marketing for two things: deals and dollars. Whether wholesaling or buying to hold, you match deals with dollars. See Chapter 3 and the Case Study in Chapter 2 on how two business partners with no prior real estate experience funded $6 million in real estate in their first 10 months using none of their own cash or credit.

Q: What if I don't have time?

I and nearly all of my students started this business part-time. In my case, I had a demanding 60 hour per week job. You have the time; you just need the right priorities and systems which I explain throughout the book. See Chapters 9 and 10.

Q: How can I pitch to investors if I don't have experience?

You use the Raising Private Money Formula. Everyone starts with no experience. You offset that by utilizing strong management companies and leverage their resume in your credibility kit. And when you present your deal to an investor thru the Raising Private Money Formula, you further position yourself as credible. See Chapter 7.

Q: How do I find the good deals?

You can find deals thru 1) listing services, 2) brokers and 3) direct mail but the two primary sources for good deals are brokers and direct mail. You can find deals in listing services but listing services are actually best for the finding the brokers with pocket listings. Direct mail is your secret weapon for marketing. See Chapter 6.

Q: How do I avoid dealing with tenants and toilets?

You are going to hire management companies who already manage hundreds of apartment units for multiple owners. And because of the revenue afforded by small apartments, versus houses, you can afford to hire good ones which focus on apartment management. Never, never, never self-manage. You are not a property manager, you are an Asset Manager. You manage the managers. See Chapter 3.

Q: Where do I start?

Since your first deal is the most critical deal in establishing your confidence, I recommend you start with small apartments (vs. mid-size or large). They close fast. Within small apartments, most choose to start with wholesaling. See Chapter 8.

Q: I want to be able to leave my job. How soon can I do that?

First, don't ever leave your current source of income for paying the bills until you have another source to replace it. You can follow the flip 1, flip 1, flip 1, hold 1 strategy where you wholesale apartments to generate active income and then cherry pick the ones to keep for passive income. You are closer than you realize right now. See Chapter 4.

Q: How do I recognize a good deal?

You evaluate commercial apartments based on the numbers, whether small, mid-size or large. You'll need to see the financials: a P&L and a Rent Roll. You don't need an automobile. You can evaluate and make offers sight unseen – even outside your own back yard. See Chapter 5.

Q: How do I know what to focus on day-by-day?

You focus on the three M's: 1) Marketing, 2) Making Offers and 3) Mindset Conditioning. You are in the marketing business, marketing for deals and dollars; two-thirds of your time needs to be devoted to marketing. See Chapters 9 and 10.

Q: I've bought real estate courses in the past but they are collecting dust. What am I doing wrong?

Seventy percent of your success is tied to mindset. The good news is that you can recondition your mindset and belief systems for new actions and habits to make money in real estate. See Chapters 9 and 10.

Q: I'm scared of speaking to a broker. What should I do?

This is a common fear. In fact, it was biggest one I had in getting started. You need to prepare a script, or use mine. A script allows you to control the conversation. There are two secrets to speaking with brokers: 1) ask high quality questions and 2) precisely describe the type of deals you are looking for. Those two items position you as knowledgeable. See Chapter 6.

Q: I'm scared of speaking to a seller. What should I do?

Just as with the fear of broker calls, use a script. It allows you to control the conversation. You can develop one or use mine. There are two secrets to speaking with sellers: 1) ask about the property first and 2) ask about the seller's situation last. Those two items position you and allow you to develop rapport. See Chapter 6.

Q: How do I structure a deal so that it is attractive to a private investor?

Use the Raising Private Money Formula. Every prospective investor wants to hear about return OF capital before they hear about return ON capital. The formula dictates how you structure the deal to satisfy this question. And it does in a way that positions you as a pro. See Chapter 7.

Q: What's the standard return model for a private investor?

There is no standard. In fact, there are three different return models to select from. You are free to structure the deal in such a way that it provides you cash flow or equity or both. First, you determine your personal financial objective and that will dictate your return structure (and the profile of the private investor you seek). See Chapter 7.

Q: What is the best entity to use in real estate?

Never, never, never buy investment real estate in your personal name. It creates personal liability for you. You want to use an LLC or a Land Trust with an LLC. You do not need an entity for wholesaling as you never take title. See the Bonus Resources Section in the back of the book.

Q: How do I protect my privacy in owning apartments?

Use a land trust. See the Bonus Resources Section in the back of the book.

Q: Do I need a real estate license for this business?

No. But avoid bird-dogging without a real estate license. The matching of sellers and buyers without a real estate license can be illegal. On the contrary, wholesaling - where you create a contract to purchase and sell your contract - requires no real estate license. You are selling a contract, not the property, by assigning your place as the buyer on the contract.

Q: What are the tax advantages of owning apartments?

Real estate is one of the great areas of tax breaks in the IRS Code. You enjoy tax benefits on both the appreciation and depreciation from apartments you own. Appreciation benefits include 1031 Exchanges and tax benefits from apartments where you live in one of the units. You can use the paper loss of depreciation to offset the tax due on your other active income. See Chapters 2 and 8, as well as the Bonus Resources Section in the back of the book.

Q: Does the Dodd-Frank Law affect owner financing in apartments like it does in houses?

Generally not. The Dodd-Frank Law was written as a result of the 2008 credit meltdown and to protect home borrowers who intend to be owner-occupants. It generally does not apply to apartments since the owner usually does not occupy the property. You can buy, sell or flip your small apartments using owner-financing. See your attorney and Chapter 2.

Q: Lance, why are you giving this information away? Aren't you concerned with creating competition?

No, I operate from an abundance mindset. The world of opportunity is larger than we can even imagine and there's more than enough to go around. Just having a slice of a slice of a slice can make you and me each a fortune. There are two things I love: deal-making and teaching. This book is an extension of my teaching. There's the possibility that by me introducing you to the world of small apartments, we may do business together some day.

Coming Up...

The remainder of the book contains a comprehensive Glossary and summary of all the Bonus Resources provided throughout the book. Use them in addition to the strategies and techniques revealed here.

Glossary

As Aristotle said, "All learning begins with definitions." Use this glossary as your guide to the jargon of the apartment industry. Each of these terms is explained in the book.

1031 Exchange: this allows investors to defer capital gains tax on an exchange of like-kind properties for business or investment purposes.

Active Income: income in which you trade your time for dollars; requires your active involvement (job)

Actuals: the actual financial performance of a property based on current and historical data, as opposed to pro-forma.

Appreciation: the increase in the value of a property, from forced appreciation and/or market appreciation.

APR: annual percentage rate, as used in mortgage interest.

Asset Manager: otherwise known as the General Manager in business; the Asset Manager selects and manages the property management company - you are an Asset Manager not a property manager.

Bad Apple Strategy: a strategy whereby you find motivated sellers in a unique way: by following the trail of bad management companies and learning which properties they manage, and then contacting those owners.

Birddog: finds a real estate lead and refers the lead to buyers who then analyze, negotiate, contract, and close the deal, upon which the birddog earns a finder's fee.

Buy Acres and Sell Lots: a strategy where you convert an apartment from *rent by the unit* to *rent by the bedroom* or bed; this raises your gross rentals.

Buy and Hold (Active Participant): a strategy where you actively find the deals, put them under contract, raise funds from private investors, close the deal as the owner and manage the management company; you are the entrepreneur.

Buy and Hold (Passive Participant): a strategy where you invest your funds in other people's projects; they own and run the property, from which you receive a passive return.

Buyer's List: a list of prospective property buyers which you grow and market your deals directly to.

Capital gains tax: a tax on capital gains, meaning the profit earned on the sale of real estate that was purchased at a cost lower than the sales price.

Capping Out a Property: the process of raising the value of a property by increasing the NOI; or receiving passive appreciation thru a decrease in market cap rates.

Cash in the Deal: the amount of cash in a deal: down payment, closing costs, rehab costs.

Cash-on-Cash Return: a percentage measure of the annual cash flow returned per dollar of Cash in the Deal.

Commercial: in the case of apartments, 5+ units. NOI is used for the valuation.

Componentizing: a powerful technique for increasing your tax benefits by accelerating the depreciation of the components of a physical building not associated with the real estate, such as the appliances.

Connect the Dots: a wholesale strategy where you find a deal and market it straight to your buyers' list.

Control: an attribute in lending transactions where the lender can exert control to get their investment back if the borrower does not perform.

Deals: a property that is under contract with terms preferential to you as the buyer, i.e. lower than market price or easy and flexible financing terms.

Debt Service: annual mortgage payment amount.

Depreciation: a paper loss on investment real estate where the IRS allows a deduction to the owner's annual tax return, based on aging of a property.

Dodd-Frank Law: the Dodd-Frank Wall Street Reform and Consumer Protection Act. This was signed into federal law by President Barack Obama in 2010, enacted in 2014, and was passed in direct response to the Great Recession to bring significant changes to lending, especially on owner-occupied properties like homes.

Dollars: when wholesaling, dollars means the End Buyer who the contract is assigned to; when buy and holding, dollars means the Private Investor who will loan money and/or credit to the entrepreneur.

Dominate and Profit: a strategy which is a variation of the Peas in a Pod strategy; you obtain enough control to dominate the property owners' association and operate the pod as a large apartment community.

Dream Busters: people who thrive on negativity and who will try to convince you that a certain plan is both worthless and foolish.

Entrepreneur: someone who pursues his or her vision using the time, talent and resources (i.e. the cash and credit) of others. Entrepreneurs provide the deals to the dollars. They are matchmakers.

Equity: the value of a property after subtracting the liens against it.

Flip: see wholesaling.

Forced Appreciation: the process of predictably raising the value of a commercial income-producing property by raising the NOI; done thru increases in rent or occupancy, and/or decreases in the expenses.

Fractured Association: a property owner association which is in financial distress.

Gentrification Riches: a strategy where you wholesale properties in areas which are undergoing gentrification and the land values are increasing.

Hard Money Lender: a private money lender that loans money based on the asset value rather than the borrower's credit; they typically charge points and higher than market interest for short-term money.

Heal and Profit: a strategy that is a variation of the Peas in a Pod strategy; you buy up the few distressed buildings in a pod and improve the buildings to raise the market value of the pod, and your buildings.

Hedge Fund: a pooling of funds by high net worth individuals for the purpose of investing large sums of capital; there is a Hedge Fund Manager who manages the fund and is paid based on performance.

High Return: illustrating a high return *relative* to the low risk of the investment.

High Ticket: a business model where you deal in high ticket priced items and earn large profit per transaction, with few transactions.

High Volume: a business model where you deal in low priced items on a high volume basis with small to modest profit per transaction, and a high volume of transactions.

Income-Based Appraisal: a method for appraising commercial income-producing properties, based on the NOI and market cap rate.

Investor: someone with cash or credit to invest into a project; investors provide the dollars to the deals.

Land Trust: a form of taking title to real estate where there is a trustee and a beneficiary and the identity of the beneficiary is private.

Law of Manifestation: a powerful law which explains how our subconscious and conscious minds interact to manifest results in our life; it tells us that our results are a function of our belief systems and habits; thereby establishing the requirement of reconditioning our internal beliefs before expecting different external results.

Large Apartments: non-specific but generally 150+ units.

Lease Option: also called a lease with the option to purchase. At the end of a specified rental period, the lessee will be given the option to purchase the property.

Leverage: the use of other people's money to maximize the return of cash in the investment.

Leverage and Velocity: a strategy where you purchase property using other people's money, raise the value thru appreciation and then use the increased equity to buy more property; velocity is doing it over and over again.

Limited Liability Company (LLC): a type of corporate entity structure for holding title in real estate; it provides asset protection and tax advantages for the individual members.

Lipstick on a Pig: industry term for raising the curb appeal of an apartment thru cosmetic improvements, in order to raise the rents and/or occupancy.

Loan to value (LTV): lenders use this term to illustrate the percentage ratio of a loan to the value of the underlying asset that was purchased.

Low Risk: an attribute of lending transactions where the lender wants to feel that the investment is low risk and secure.

Marketing: the purpose of any business.

Mid-size Apartments: non-specific but generally 31-150 units.

Mindset: a positive or negative state of mind that attracts certain things into one's life; a belief system of what's possible for you.

Money before the Sale: a strategy where you offer products beside real estate deals to the clients on your buyers' list – such as information products.

Net Operating Income (NOI): an apartment's annual revenue less expenses; expenses do not include the mortgage payments.

Net Worth: your assets less your liabilities; in apartments it's equity in your buildings.

Non-Recourse Financing: apartment financing where there is no personal guarantor to the loan; the property is the sole collateral so that in the event of default, the lender's only remedy is to take back the property with "no recourse" to the borrower.

Occupancy: the percent of occupied units in an apartment (physical occupancy).

Off-Market Deals: property that is not actively listed for sale by the owner directly or thru an agent; there is no competition from other buyers or any middle-person as the agent.

OPM: other people's money.

Own Nothing, Control Everything: a strategy where you exercise a master lease option on an apartment; you receive control and financial gain without owning the property.

Owner-Financing: a condition when the owner sells a property and takes back some or all their sales price as installment payments rather than up-front cash.

Partner for Profit: a strategy to find motivated sellers by offering to partner with owners to improve their property using your money.

Passive Income: income for which one does not actively work; mailbox money.

Peas in a Pod: a strategy for buying or flipping individual duplexes, triplexes or four-plexes (peas), all within the same neighborhood (pod) of similar buildings.

Pocket Listing: a property listing that is privately held by a broker and not on any public listing service.

Points: a form of prepaid interest; one point is equal to one percent of the loan amount.

Polish the Diamond: a strategy where you buy performing apartments and the only value play is to "buy it right," using the financials.

Predisposed: investors who are already interested in investing in real estate; they are looking for projects to invest in.

Productivity Timer: a 60 minute timer that is used to maintain focus; when operating under this timer, you are only allowed to work on your marketing and to make offers.

Profit and Loss Report (P&L): a financial report for an apartment which shows the Revenue, Expenses and NOI for each month and YTD for the previous (trailing) 12 months.

Pro-Forma: the projected financial performance of an apartment, as opposed to actuals.

Property Management Company: company responsible for the daily operation of the apartment, including leasing, maintenance, rent collection, marketing, bill paying and accounting.

Property Owner Association: an association of all the owners of property in a neighborhood, responsible for the upkeep of the common areas and directed by a board of owners.

Recourse Financing: real estate financing where there is a personal guarantor to the loan; the property is the collateral as well as the guarantor's own assets, which the lender can pursue in the event of default. Note the borrower and guarantor may be different entities or persons.

Refinance: the process of placing a new loan on a property to replace an existing mortgage – whether to lock in a lower interest rate or to pull some of the equity out of the property as cash.

Rent Roll: an apartment report which lists all units and shows by unit: the resident's name, the amount of rent charged and collected, the move-in date, the lease expiration, the security deposit amount and any balance due.

Residential: houses and in the case of small apartments, 2-4 units (duplexes, triplexes and four-plexes); valuation is based on "comparables" just like houses.

REO: real estate owned; this is property owned by a bank or other lender after a foreclosure.

Reticular Activating System: a network of nerves in the brain that mediate a person's consciousness.

Self-directed IRA: a type of IRA where the owner can select where to invest the fund, including real estate.

Seller-Financing: see Owner Financing.

Single flip: the most basic strategy in which one finds a deal, finds a buyer, and flips the contract.

Small Apartments: non-specific but generally 2-30 units

Special Needs: a strategy where you market an apartment for rent to special needs groups that will pay a premium rent.

Specialized Knowledge: the "how to" knowledge of a business.

Short Sale: a sale of a property in which the proceeds are not enough to pay the debts secured by liens against the property; the lien holders agree to release their liens and accept less than they are owed.

Starving Crowd: a strategy for wholesaling small apartments to the largest buying group of small apartments: single-family home landlords.

Syndicator: see Buy and Hold (Active Participant).

Systems: the collection of processes, technology and people for running a true business – without the active participation of the owner.

Triple Net Lease (NNN): a form of commercial lease where the tenant pays the rent plus all expenses for the operation of the property.

Uncle Sam: a strategy for leveraging the IRS tax advantages of owning apartments.

Value Plays: recognized opportunities to increase the value of an apartment thru forced appreciation or "buying it right."

Virtual Assistant: an assistant who works from a location remote from you; they could be located anywhere in the world.

Wholesaling: the strategy for placing a property under contract to purchase and then assigning the contract to another end buyer who pays you an assignment fee; you never take title.

Wrap-around Mortgage: a type of financing where you buy or sell a property with the existing mortgage left in place; the new mortgage "wraps around" the existing mortgage.

Summary of Resources and FREE Offer

Here is a summary of the Bonus Resources referenced in the book as well as my offer for a *complimentary* planning session to get you started.

Complimentary Planning Session:

You have what it takes in this book to get started and I want to get you on the right path to action. You can receive a FREE phone consultation to establish your plan for your first 12 months. Apply here:

www.BMSABook.com/plan

Here are all the other multimedia Bonus Resources referenced in the book, organized alphabetically:

Apartment Business Tools:

- Apartment Deal Analysis Cheat Sheet
  www.BMSAbook.com/sheet

- Performance Dashboard
  www.BMSABook.com/dashboard

Reports:

- 20 Reasons Why You Should Use an LLC for Real Estate
  www.BMSABook.com/20llc

Success Story Interviews:

- $13,750 Made Flipping an Apartment with Snakes
  www.BMSABook.com/snakes

- $24,000 from Her First Small Apartment Flip
  www.BMSABook.com/triplexes

- $255,000 Equity Gain with Forced Appreciation
  www.BMSABook.com/forced

- Bad Management Makes for Good Deal
  www.BMSAbook.com/rehab

- Circle of Champions Roundtable Interview
  www.BMSABook.com/roundtable

- House Flipper Doubles Profits with Four-Plex
  www.BMSABook.com/double

- Part-time Flipper Makes $26,500 in 60 Days
  www.BMSABook.com/peas

- The Secret to 100% Owner Financing
  www.BMSABook.com/ken

- Window Installer Makes $60,000 On First Deal
  www.BMSABook.com/60k

Webinar Trainings:

- 7 Keys to Building a Real Estate Empire
  www.BMSAbook.com/7keys

- How to Be an Apartment Turnaround Specialist
  www.BMSABook.com/turn

- How to Invest in Real Estate Using IRA's
  www.BMSABook.com/ira

- How to Make Big Money in Small Apartments
  www.BMSABook.com/bmsa

- How to Present to Private Money Investors
  www.BMSABook.com/present

- How to Raise Huge Money in Today's Economy
  www.BMSABook.com/rpm

- How to Wholesale Apartments
  www.BMSABook.com/flip

- Land Trusts Made Simple
  www.BMSABook.com/trusts

- Real Estate Tax Strategies Your CPA Doesn't Know
  www.BMSABook.com/taxes

- The Hidden Power of LLC's
  www.BMSABook.com/llc

- The Whole Truth About Real Estate Investing
  www.BMSABook.com/truth

Affiliate Information for Money Before the Sale

- Become My Affiliate
  www.BMSAbook.com/affiliate

How to Reach Lance Edwards

The author, Lance Edwards, is available for a limited number of speaking engagements and consulting assignments. He also has a selection of training programs and mentoring programs. For information, contact Lance Edwards at:

First Cornerstone Group, LLC
1345 Campbell Rd, Suite 200
Houston, TX 77055
713-476-0102
ClientCare@fcgllc.com

Disclaimer

Specific examples, case studies, and general content within these pages do not embody the average user experience. In actuality, the "average user" consists of many individuals, some of which may purchase our service and never actually use the advice or product.

Monetary results as well as yearly income are based on a host of factors. There is no way to know how well any individual will perform, not knowing that individual's background, business sense, practices, or general work ethic. With this in mind, we cannot guarantee the results of those who have succeeded using our methods.

Readers cannot assume the results that will happen when using this program. The case studies mentioned in this collaboration do not represent or guarantee any results that have already occurred or may occur in the immediate future.

Instead, the case studies represent *what is possible*, given the advice within these pages. Since each case is so unique, reported results vary and most of the results are never actually recorded. Additional information includes pricing, market conditions, personal initiatives, and many, many other factors.

Earnings mentioned in this book are based off specific examples or estimations of what could be earned, using these methods. However, that does not mean there is any specific assurance that your figures will be the same as the figures in this book. Readers must accept the risk of disappointment.

Real estate businesses and their earnings come with their own unknown risks like any business. Therefore, making decisions based on specific examples in this book should be performed with the understanding that these results will most likely not be the same as the example provided.

Always use caution when seeking advice from professionals or those claiming to be professionals. Speak with an accountant, lawyer, or professional advisor before acting on advice provided from those individuals you do not personally know.

This disclaimer means that you agree that our company is not responsible for the success or failure of your business decisions, relating to information presented by our company, products or services. This notice refers to "you," "your," "reader," and "user," meaning "you the reader." In regards to "we" or "our," we are referring to Lance Edwards or First Cornerstone Group, LLC.

Made in the USA
Columbia, SC
04 November 2018